THE I'M GRAND MAMUAL

Cork-born **PJ Kirby** and **Kevin Twomey** are co-hosts of popular weekly podcast *I'm Grand Mam*, which has accrued millions of listens to date. As well as being podcasters, the pair have also written two comedy shows, *Pure Brazen* (2019) and *Glory Holy* (2021), that have toured the UK and Ireland to sold-out audiences. They have been featured in many publications, including the *Irish Times*, *Irish Examiner*, *Sunday Independent*, *Grazia*, *Vogue* and *GCN*. They're also no strangers to TV, regularly appearing on *The Late Late Show*, *Ireland AM* and *The Six O'Clock Show*. PJ currently lives in Dublin and Kevin is still in London, but there's no separating these two; more often than not, you'll find them together, working on their next project.

A STUNNING GUIDE TO TAKING LIFE IN YOUR STRIDE

THE I'M GRAND MAMUAL

PJ Kirby & Kevin Twomey

Gill Books

Gill Books
Hume Avenue
Park West
Dublin 12
www.gillbooks.ie

Gill Books is an imprint of M.H. Gill and Co.

9780717198870

Designed by Bartek Janczak
Illustrations by Alannah Calvert
Printed and bound in Great Britain by CPI Group (UK) Ltd,
Croydon, CRO 4YY
This book is typeset in 11 on 17pt, Minion Pro.

*The paper used in this book comes from the wood pulp of
sustainably managed forests.*

A CIP catalogue record for this book is available from the
British Library.

5 4 3 2 1

PJ

To my dad, thank you for always supporting
me in my life choices, even when you didn't
fully understand them. I wish you could have
seen where they led. This one's for you.

Pat Kirby, 1947–2013

Kevin

To my dad, who always told me how proud he
was. I know he would be particularly proud
of this.

Jerry Twomey, 1958–2022

Contents

Hey Girlies ...

I'm Kevin.

And I'm PJ.

And together we've written *The I'm Grand Mamual*!

Woooooo!

We're published authors! Can you cope? When we first got asked about writing a book we were like, 'OMG absolutely!' We were imagining how stunning the finished product would look on a coffee table in our respective houses and Kevin was ready already updating his Tinder bio to include 'author'. We thought of the press tour, the book signings and how much of a pinch-me moment it would be to walk past a bookshop in Cork and spot our faces in the window gracing the cover of our very own publication and we started fighting over fonts. But the process has been so much more than that. Writing this book has been such a joy: recounting the journey we've both been on together over the last few years and recalling formative tales from our childhood, finding comfort in how far we've both come and thinking about how happy our younger selves would be to see us living our lives authentically and on our own terms.

Kevin: The pair of us met in 2013 when I was studying in UCC and PJ was teaching hip-hop classes for the dance society on campus. Despite my background being more modern and jazz-based, I went to PJ's class to see what all the fuss was about and I had such a scream. He taught a routine to Rihanna's 'Cockiness (Love It)' and though I felt completely out of my comfort zone, I didn't care. I think we both felt a bit of a connection to each other that day, perhaps because we were both closeted gay men who loved dancing and we saw a bit of ourselves in each other – or maybe PJ fancied me a bit. Who knows?

PJ: Now, I definitely didn't fancy Kev, but I was up to ninety when he came to class because I knew straight away he was a flaming homosexual and I was panicked that he would see that I was too. Anyway, the fear quickly subsided and we got so friendly that year I asked him to MC the fundraiser I was hosting to support me going to dance college in London. If there's one thing that boy can do, it's host a party. He was fab.

Kevin: The day after the fundraiser, I spotted him in town sporting a pair of expensive Air Jordans, which he insists weren't purchased with the money he had raised the day before. (I suppose this doesn't really have anything to do with the story of how we met but I just love telling people that it happened.)

PJ: I've never worn Air Jordans in my life, by the way. I moved to London that September and Kev followed the year after but was living in Essex so we lost touch for a bit, both busy doing our own thing, but moved in together three years later when Kev graduated.

Kevin: Initially I slept on his pull-out couch for three months before we could find a bigger gaff, and though my back was broken from sleeping on a mattress that was the thickness of a Ryvita cracker, I was happy to be reunited again with my best friend.

PJ: When we moved into our tiny terraced house in Stratford, living in a gaff where I didn't have to climb over Kev's bed to get to the fridge in the morning was a welcome change. We loved having people over for dinners, cups of Barry's tea we'd smuggled over from trips home and pre-drinks ahead of a big, gay night out. The idea for *I'm Grand Mam* came about in January 2019 on a trip to Budapest for my birthday. After a few glasses of red wine on our Ryanair flight, we asked the air hostess for a pen and started planning our first episode of *I'm Grand Mam* on the back of a sick bag as we crossed over Europe, 10,000 feet in the air.

Kevin: We arrived back in London with big ambitions and a touch of food poisoning, but that didn't deter us. The microphone we had ordered from Amazon was waiting for us so we felt obliged to follow through with our plan. Otherwise, it would have been a waste of £50. Sure, it would have been rude not to. And now the rest is history. We never anticipated the podcast getting so popular and achieving the success that it has.

PJ: It's been a bit of a whirlwind, girlies. Thanks to the success of the pod, we've been able to perform all over the UK and Ireland, shoot stunning campaigns, and be featured in loads of glam publications. We were even mentioned in *Vogue*, which is mad. Okay, it's not like we went for coffee with Anna Wintour, it was a tiny mention – but we'll take it!

Kevin: In 2022, we did a live UK and Ireland tour, performing to sold-out venues in Cork, Dublin, Galway, Belfast, London and Edinburgh. We also appeared on *The Late Late Show*, and we were weak because our mammies got to be there too.

PJ & Kevin: But for us, the most rewarding thing about starting *I'm Grand Mam* has been bringing a smile to people's faces. We're constantly getting messages from Irish expats from all around the world telling us of how we've helped cure them of their homesickness with our nostalgic tales and our self-deprecating humour, all delivered in our cutting Cork accents. We've also been completely overwhelmed by messages from LGBTQ+ people who've shared with us that through our honest and open conversations about our lived experiences as gay men, we've helped them celebrate their queerness.

Now we're going from podcasters to authors and creating *The I'm Grand Mamual.* Think of this book as the big-sister advice book for the gays and girlies of Ireland. This book is a celebration of identity and a guide to living life as your most authentic self. Using the sage words of our mams as the starting point for each chapter, and showcasing how we've applied this advice to our own lives, we're hoping to give some direction and guidance to others that need it. As out and proud queer people we can throw away the rule book as we're already going against the grain of societal norms. Hopefully, this book will give others who are struggling to fully accept themselves the encouragement to follow the way of the gays. As queer people, we have a shared experience of feeling like the outcasts, the odd ones out. This book is for anyone who has ever been made to feel like they don't belong and to highlight that there is strength, beauty and unity in our otherness.

Meet the Mammies

Nuala PJ'S MAM

Phil KEVIN'S MAM

Nuala and Phil are two icons in their own right. They are the embodiment of what it means to be an Irish mammy; patient, kind, quick-witted, altruistic, tea-loving, compassionate, weather-obsessed women. They gave birth to two absolute legends, so cheers for that. Our mams are at the heart of our podcast and the origins of the title *I'm Grand Mam* unsurprisingly stems from our relationship with them. Irish mammies are worriers by nature – 'You better wear your jacket or you'll get pneumonia!' 'Put that down, you don't know where it's been!' 'Did you dry your ears after your shower?' – and our mams are no different. This anxiety escalates when you move away from home as a mam loses her ability to have regular surveillance over your life and because she believes that there are weirdos out there in the big bad world that don't exist in your local parish. When we moved to London we were met with constant messages, phone calls and FaceTimes from our frantic mammies, who would always ask if we were okay. In an effort to not cause further fretting, our response would always be the same: 'I'm grand, Mam.'

Our mams have been our mentors, shaping us into the individuals we are today with their percipient pointers and their enlightenment, which has informed a lot of the decisions we've made in our lives. As we're so generous, we didn't want to keep all this insight and information to ourselves – no gatekeeping here, girlies – and decided to get our listeners in on the guidance by giving our mams an entire section to themselves in the podcast, known as 'Mam Knows Best'. We encouraged listeners in need of some words of wisdom to submit questions for Nuala and Phil. Initially, we read out their responses but once our mams mastered the art of recording a WhatsApp voice note, we knew it was time to give them their moment in the spotlight and have them feature directly in the podcast, and *The I'm Grand Mamual* is an extension of this.

This book is a love letter to our mams.

Thank you, Phil and Nuala.

AN A–Z OF IRISH MAMMIES

Irish mammies really are in a league of their own. They're as sharp as scissors and funny without even trying. And though no two Irish mammies are the same, there are certain quips, comments and characteristics that are synonymous with the beloved Irish matriarch and we've compiled an A–Z of our favourites below:

A is for Anthony: The patron saint of lost things and the unofficial patron saint of Irish mammies.

B is for 'Bye, bye, bye, g'wan, bye, bye': The obligatory phone-call sign-off for mams and how we finish every episode of the podcast.

C is for candles: Irish mammies are always lighting candles for people.

D is for Daniel O'Donnell: The Harry Styles of our mammies' generation. 'Oh wow, Daniel is here!'

E is for *Eastenders*: Because what's a mam without her soaps?

F is for flat 7up: Prescribed by all mammies everywhere to help cure any ailment.

G is for 'G'wan away au' that': Uttered by mams if you're talking nonsense or if they don't believe you.

H is for the heating: Irish mams are always frozen and you can win them over by offering to run upstairs and turn on the heating.

I is for inhaling: Irish mams are the only sector of the population known to inhale as they speak.

J is for jacket: If you're leaving the house your mam won't let you go outside without mentioning your jacket, irrespective of the season.

K is for Knock: A place of pilgrimage. Holy water from Knock is to be reserved for special occasions only, like blessing a new car.

L is for LOL: They write it at the end of text messages thinking it means 'lots of love' and we love them for it.

M is for 'Make sure the immersion's off x'.

N is for nosy: In a good way. Some might say inquisitive.

O is for Orla Kiely: A figure revered amongst Irish mammies. If in doubt about what gift to get an Irish mam, Orla Kiely bits are always a solid option.

P is for potpourri: A mixture of dried plant materials, which didn't really serve any purpose and were found in most Irish residential settings in the 90s.

Q is for 'Quick, help me take in the washing. It's going to lash!'

R is for Rip.ie: Website most visited by Irish mams.

S is for she: 'Who's "she", the cat's mother?'

T is for tea: Tea courses through the veins of every Irish mammy.

U is for 'Unless you want a kidney infection, you better get up those stairs and put on a pair of socks.'

V is for vaping: Kevin's mam loves her vape.

W is for wooden spoon: Mostly used for baking but there's also the threat of a smack of it if you're acting the eejit.

Y is for yoke: 'That's an awful weird yoke, where'd you get that?'

Z is for zooming in to photos on a phone and asking who the person is.

Now that you've had your lesson in Irish mammies, we're going to get you up to speed with some of the iconic phrases and expressions that make up a Cork person's vernacular. Language is a beautiful thing, especially when it's coming from the mouth of someone from the rebel county.

CORK SLANG

Allergic: A strong expression of dislike. 'My boss asked me to come in to work an hour early in the morning and I couldn't be more allergic.'

Bazzer: A haircut. 'Look at the state of your man's bazzer – it looks like he got in a fight with a lawnmower.'

Bulb off: Two things that look the same. 'I get bad vibes from the new postman – he's the bulb off that Hannibal Lecter fella.'

Flah: To have sexual intercourse and also used to denote a good-looking person. 'That Paul Mescal lad with the chain is some flah.'

Gatting: Drinking alcohol. 'Are we going gatting in yours first or what's the story?'

Haunted: Extremely lucky. 'It didn't rain once down in Ballylickey. We were haunted with the weather.'

Lamp: To look at someone. 'She was lamping me all night, so I asked her if she wanted to go to Fast Al's for a slice of pizza.'

Langers: Extremely intoxicated. Also used as a term for a penis. 'He was so langers at Michelle's wedding last weekend he got his langer out in the photo booth.'

Lapsy pa: Someone who's a bit all over the place/clumsy. 'We were only supposed to go out for a few jars, but sure, I was lapsy pa walking home.'

Rasa: Raspberry cordial. 'Two double vodkas and rasa, please!'

Snake: Sneak. 'I spent a fortune on my top for tonight so I'm going to have to snake a naggin into the club.'

Mockeeah: Pretend, fictional, fake. 'He said he was getting me the new Dyson hairdryer for Christmas but he only got me a mockeeah one off the back of a van.'

Weak: Obsessed with something. 'I love the coffee in Some Dose and I'm weak for all the lads that work there, they're pure sound.'

Up to ninety: To be stressed out because you have a lot on your plate. 'I was up to ninety because the queue was so long in Penney's and I was meant to be getting my nails done at three.'

→ ONE ←

Growing Up Gay

'To each their own.'

NUALA KIRBY

PJ

The Big Big Movie made me gay

It's a Saturday night and I'm just after hounding down a plate of chicken nuggets and chips chased with a pint of milk, the only type of meal I would eat that year. I'm the youngest of seven and was a picky eater as a child so I think my parents were just like, *Feck it, let him eat nuggs for a year, we're wrecked from raising the rest of them*. We're hurrying to wash our plates and get the microwave popcorn ready before the Big Big Movie comes on RTÉ. (This was before you could pause or record the telly, so timing was crucial.) After losing a fight with my sister Lindsey for the good seat, we settled in and the film began. This week it was *The Full Monty*. If you don't know the plot, it's basically about a group of lads forming a striptease group after being laid off from the factory they all worked at. A vintage *Magic Mike*, if you will. Bit of a riskier choice for RTÉ, and I was definitely too young to be watching it, but here we were. Girlies, my little adolescent heart was up to ninety. I was weak for the lead, Gaz, and once they started stripping in the Garda outfits I didn't know where to look. It was all very innocent of course, but that strange feeling would pop up every now and then going forward. When I looked at the packaging in the male underwear department, when Syed and Christian kissed in *Eastenders*, one time in Costa del Sol when I saw two men holding hands. I'd get giddy butterflies in my stomach that I knew I had to hide. I knew I couldn't be gay, you see. Even though I wasn't completely sure what gay meant, I just knew it was a bad thing used to insult someone. To laugh at them. So, I pushed these feelings down and learned to ignore them. From then on, I knew I had a secret that nobody could find out, so I put measures in place to make sure it wouldn't happen. Maybe that's why gays are so good at PR, because we've been spinning the truth since we could talk.

Growing up, we'd spend Friday nights in The Residence Bar across the street from my gaff. All of our neighbours would be there with their kids so it was perfect because my mam and dad could have a few drinks with their friends while the kids were kept entertained by the touch machine in the corner as we drank our body weight in rasa. My friend Jordan's parents owned the bar, so he could snake us a few packs of Tayto on the sly, which was fab. You could also get a stunning toastie, and I'm sorry now, but every bar should be legally required to have a toastie maker on the premises, in my opinion.

Anyway, we would be having the time of our lives but, at a certain point in the night, I'd have to get strategic. The older men would be after having a few scoops of stout by now and political correctness would go out the window. I don't even think we knew what being PC was back then. They would go from a terrible joke about women in the kitchen to a racist one before coming for the gays. The limp wrists would come out, and they would parody the camp man who cuts their wives' hair. I never understood the joke. I just knew I never wanted to be the punchline, so I kept the head down.

Barbies, bisexuals and Britney

I'd hide any behaviour that could be seen as gay. I'd play Barbies with my neighbour Sarah but carry them to her house in a Dunnes Bag for Life so nobody could see them. Looking back, obviously I know that playing with Barbies doesn't make you gay, but back then I felt like anything that fell outside of what 'normal boys' do needed to be done away from the public eye. Eventually, hiding these parts of myself became second nature – and I was actually unreal at it. Sure, I'd slip up a little from time to time and have to talk my way out of why I knew all the words to 'Oops! ... I Did It Again' by Britney Spears, but that's where having sisters came in handy. Like, I only watched *Sabrina the Teenage Witch* because Lindsey liked it, obviously.

It's difficult to explain, but as I came into my teens I pushed that butterfly feeling so far down I forgot about it sometimes. Like a messy pile of clothes you shove under your bed. You know it's still there but it doesn't cross your mind as much. I kissed girls and had girlfriends that I fell in love with, but not the passionate, free-flowing love that I know now. It was more like the love you would have for a best friend. As I grew older, I would hate when these annoying butterflies would come back. I remember one morning I woke up from a dream where I had a big ride of a boyfriend and we were just kissing on a couch for the whole thing. I went and looked at myself in the mirror with tears in my eyes, so angry with myself for having these feelings. The urge came over me to punch the mirror and watch my reflection shatter, which, looking back on it, is ridiculously dramatic and so camp that I should have accepted my fate then and there. Honestly, though, I was nowhere near ready to address my queerness, and who could blame me? Homosexuality was only decriminalised in Ireland the year I was born but, although it was legal, everyone wasn't running to buy rainbow flags to hang outside their windows.

When I moved to London to start dance college at 20 years of age, I was still in the closet. During orientation, my jaw was on the floor, girls. Every letter from the alphabet mafia was in the room with me. Lesbians, gays, bisexuals, trans people and everything in between sang and danced around the halls of the academy in Angel. The butterflies were back, but I felt less of a need to push them down. I wasn't ready to let them fly out of the closet, but it was a welcome relief not to have to shoo them away. I was in the academy for roughly three months when I got a call from home that my dad had had a fall. I was rushed onto the next Ryanair flight back home to be by his side. When my sister was also called back from Australia, I knew that it wasn't looking good. The next few days were a bit of a blur but, basically, my dad was in a coma and it was only a matter of time before he went. We lived in the hospital for those few days. Time stopped for us, but the world kept going. One day, Lindsey and I went for a walk in Wilton Shopping Centre to have a break from the sanitised hospital hallways, and we hated everyone that walked past us. 'How dare they be having a laugh shopping when our dad is dying a couple of metres away?' I said, half-joking but also kind of serious. For them it was just a normal day but for us our world was changing forever. Anyway, if I threw you a dirty look in Wilton in 2013, I apologise, but we were going through it.

It's now or never

The time came to say our goodbyes and we all took turns of going into the room. For some reason, I was by myself. Nobody trains you how to say goodbye to a parent, so I was a bit awkward. Everyone kept telling me that hearing is the last sense to go so he would be able to hear what I'm saying. I started with the usual checklist: *You were a great dad, I love you, will miss you, etc*. But then I felt like I was acting, reading a monologue of what a son should be saying to his dad, so I started to speak about whatever popped into my head. I talked about the time we spent together as he drove me to rugby, having chats both shallow and deep that I'll always remember. About how he used to always grab my mam in the kitchen for a dance and how I romanticise the memory by setting it at golden hour. He'd spin my mam around and they'd laugh as she stumbled over his feet. As I was telling these stories, I could feel the butterflies bubbling up inside me. *Tell him. It's now or never. Hearing is the last to go.* Before I knew it, I blurted out words I thought would never come out of my mouth: 'I'm gay, Dad.' Panic ensued and I started to ramble. 'I'm gay and I wasn't going to say anything. I actually was never going to come out. I'm not sure why I said it. I suppose this whole experience is making me think life is too short and, in the grand scheme of things, who I hook up with shouldn't really matter. Jesus, I shouldn't be talking about hooking up, but here we are. So, yeah, I'm gay and I hope you still love me.'

Now, I don't know what I expected to happen next. He wasn't going to spring out of the bed and be like, *Werk, bitch, let's grab some brunch*, but I was just sitting there in silence, sweating. I could hear my heartbeat in my ears as I kissed him on the forehead and said 'I love you' for the last time. Cue my journey of navigating grief and coming to terms with my sexuality. The vibes were on the floor, girlies. Losing my dad really did change the way I viewed the world. It's difficult to explain unless you've lost someone so close to you, but I don't think you ever truly heal from a loss like that – you just learn how to live with it. You also learn to see it in other people and they see it in you. They just get it without having to put words to the feeling. It's shit, but as B*Witched said in their 1998 smash hit, 'c'est la vie'. As life moves on, you learn how to look back on the memories you have with them and smile. It still hurts, but I think it helps to tell stories about them so their memory lives on.

After that, it was time to come out to people who weren't walking towards a bright light.

Fingers crossed they'll be more receptive. Bleak, I know but if you don't laugh you'll cry. Anyone who's ever come out knows you have to do it like a million times and it's exhausting but, considering that my first one was the most dramatic thing in the world, I tried to make the other ones as light-hearted as possible. Having a few drinks in my sister Elaine's garden, I said to my mam, 'Jesus, did you hear who came out as gay?' When she turned to me and said, 'Ooh, who?' I threw in, 'Me!' – which in hindsight was probably a bit too casual. She then added that she was okay with it as long as I was happy. My mam was actually giving a performance that would have swept the Oscars if caught on film. In years to come, I'd find out that she struggled to come to terms with the fact that I was gay. She worried, as most parents do, that life would be more difficult for me. I'm grateful that my mam drew upon what I can only assume were childhood drama lessons in that moment, though. I don't think I could have taken anything but complete acceptance from the one parent who could respond to me. My heart goes out to members of the queer community who aren't as lucky.

Another one of my – should we call them outings? – was when I was watching a film with my besties, Dylan and Jordan. A gay couple came on screen and I said, 'Oh, there's me!' and then I basically ran out of the house before they could respond, only for us to meet up later and me to get slagged – not for being gay but for being pure weird and awkward about it.

Coming out became so tedious that I seriously considered renting a billboard in the middle of Cork City that would read, 'PJ Kirby is a flaming homosexual', followed by 'Form a queue, boys' and my mobile number to make use of the exposure.

Lost in London

Twenty-one, back in London, lost: those were the vibes. I didn't feel at all stable. I wasn't dealing with my grief. I dropped out of dance college and tried to navigate the gay scene in London. Grindr was downloaded, my hair was bleached and I'd bought my first douche, even though I didn't know how to use it yet and definitely just gave myself the runs. I'd go to random hook-ups and try my hand at dating, living my big, gay *Sex and the City* fantasy. There were about two to three years of me as a baby lamb learning how to walk. Dancing in Heaven nightclub, riding boys I'd never see again and having a summer romance with a guy from Vegas. Throughout this time, the majority of my friends were straight and, although I loved them, I longed for a group of friends who understood what it was like to be a big homo.

Kevin and I started hanging out more in his final year at musical theatre college. We knew each other from back home, but he was based in Essex for three years, so I didn't see him much. But in his final year he would get the train into London so we could go on nights out. This is when I really began to explore my queerness on a deeper level. We would go to Dollar Baby in Bethnal Green, and it was a gay boy's dream. I still remember our first night there: we were just in the door and a drag queen jumped from the second-storey balcony onto a strip pole and landed in the splits as the crowd erupted. We were gagged!

When Kev graduated, he moved in and stayed on my couch. We really were each other's cheerleaders, helping to begin to shed the shame and Catholic guilt from our childhood. Obviously, we were like a double act exploring the London queer scene, but it was deeper than that. We swapped stories about growing up gay in Cork and read the same books that addressed the trauma of having to come out. Honestly, I feel like Kev acted like my armbands as I progressed from the shallow end of the gay pool in London into the deeper, more openly queer waters. He made me feel so safe and secure, and that meant I could take risks, be brave and completely accept who I was – and that's just one of the reasons why I'm mad about him.

Queer and proud

As I write this today I feel like the younger version of me is a completely different person, scared and muted. Now I'm unapologetically queer and so proud of it. Contrary to what your mad far-right cousin posts about on Facebook, being queer isn't a choice. We're born this way, as my girl Gaga reiterates over an iconic beat.

But if it was a choice, I'd choose it one hundred times over. The queer community I've around me now is made up of some of the most loving individuals I've ever met. As we progress as a society we're learning that sexuality is a spectrum. Nobody is 100 per cent gay or straight. That's why I identify more as queer now. It's more of an umbrella term for people who are not heterosexual or cisgender, and I think I could have benefitted from that terminology as a child. It felt so black and white when I was younger. Back then, if you were a man who liked another man you were gay, whereas now that's not the case. You could be bi or pan, for example. But prejudice will always exist and we still have a long way to go. Just like our queer ancestors fought for us, we need to fight for the next generation of queer kids. Something my friend Lisa Connell said on a panel will always stick with me: 'Progress is not linear.' We can't just rest on what we've achieved as a community, as things can go backwards – just look at what's happening in America. There is work to be done, but we can start off by adopting the 'to each their own' mentality that Nuala Kirbs has lived by. As long as people are not hurting themselves or others, let them be happy. Life is difficult enough. But even with that beautiful outlook being taught to me at a young age, it still took me a while to live by those words.

Kevin

Papa don't preach

For as long as I can remember, I've been quite sensitive. A distinct softness. As a child, I resented it because it set me apart. Defunct and damaging tropes of boys being brave and liking the colour blue and not crying were at odds with the child that I was. And there wasn't really any way of hiding it. I would try and shy away from it but ultimately I would end up telling on myself when it came to posing for a photograph, or when I opted to skip instead of run when we played chase in the estate, or when I was the first person to compliment my mam when she got her hair done. Actually, I was typically the first person to compliment most of my friends' mams when they'd return from Peter Marks with their colour, cut and curly blow-dry. You're welcome, girls.

Though I was shy, I loved to sing and dance and perform, and my mam and dad always embraced and encouraged my artistic notions. For my birthday one year, they got me a karaoke machine and I honestly nearly lost the will to live. I was obsessed with it. And the best part about it was that my siblings weren't confident enough to give it a go in front of everyone, so I never had to share. Bliss! It came with one cassette tape and only had four songs to choose from, and you best believe that I rinsed and rehearsed and repeated those tracks for all they were worth. My favourite of the selection was Madonna's 'Papa Don't Preach'. Me with a microphone, aged seven, singing about an unplanned pregnancy – what a moment in pop-culture history! It's a crime that video footage doesn't exist of me doing my best Madge, but I know little Kevin was just happy to have had his moment in the spotlight.

Performance became a way of expression for me and also a diversion, a means of slipping away from expectations and embracing my eccentricities by playing different characters. One Christmas, I got a magic set from Santa. I hadn't included this on my list, so once again my parents were taking my lead and fostering a space where I was encouraged to create and be myself. I practised all the tricks until I could pull them off with precision and then I would put on a show out in my back garden for the other children in the estate and charge them for admittance. Molly-Mae would have been proud. I loved the show *Taina* on Nickelodeon and would dress up my sister Sarah and teach her routines that we would perform as Blue Mascara, the girl group from the series. She wasn't great and couldn't hold down a harmony line, so I had to do a lot of the heavy lifting, but I parked my ego for the sake of the band.

One Sunday when we were at St Columba's Church, there was a call-out for altar servers and I remember thinking I had to be one. Not because I was mad for mass but because it essentially provided me with another platform for performance. Everyone would have their eyes on me while I belted out the lyrics to all the best holy bops, like 'The Cloud's Veil' or 'Gloria in Excelsis Deo', while I served in my gorge vestments, my hair immaculately parted and combed over to the side. I ate the communion and left no crumbs.

TOP *ALIVE-O* BOPS

Alive-O was a religious workbook that we grew up with in school that taught us important values like love and respect for one another – but most importantly it taught us some of the biggest, most pious anthems of our generation. The producers of the songs had bills to pay when they got into the studio and laid down these tracks. Here's a ranking of my favourites:

8. **'Monday Morning':** The song that tried to trick us into thinking that Monday to Friday are the best days of the week because we're in school, and I 100 per cent bought into it.

7. **'Body Clock':** This song slapped. If it were to be re-leased today with an accompanying dance routine it would go viral on TikTok.

6. **'The Passover Song (Baruch Atah Adonai, Eloheinu)':** This Hebrew hymn hit hard and had us all hooked. I didn't know what we were singing about but, girl, I was living.

5. **'What's the Story?':** David Guetta has been real quiet since this banger dropped.

4. **'Connected':** All the other greatest love songs of all time pale in comparison. Adele who?

3. **'Twelve Tribes of Israel':** I couldn't tell you my PPS number but you best believe I can rattle off Reuben, Benjamin, Judah, Levi, Zebulun, Gad, Asher, Issachar,

Joseph, Simeon, Naphtali and Dan without any hums or hesitations.

2. **'A Song to St Brigid':** This song had no business being this much of a belter. If I'm in control of the aux lead at an afters you know this song is going to be queued.

1. **'Circle of Friends':** Undisputedly in the top spot. The song is so ingrained into my consciousness that even if a satellite fell from the sky and landed on my head and I developed amnesia, I would still be able to recall the lyrics.

I didn't hyper-fixate on my quirks but there was an awareness there that I was an outlier. In an all-boys national school, my idiosyncrasies became a bit more conspicuous. There was one boy in my class with whom I became infatuated. I was a child, so of course it was all very innocent, but I just remember being drawn to him and wanting to be his friend so badly. Once when my teacher was assigning seats, she asked if anyone wanted to sit next to this particular individual and, my god, did I have my *lámha suas*. My arm nearly shot out of its socket I was so set on sharing a desk with this boy who I was too nervous to speak to at playtime. But despite me sitting next to him for an entire term and sharing all my gel pens, he committed the ultimate act of primary-school betrayal by not inviting me to his party at Leisureplex. No Q-Zar or Viennetta for me.

Don't phunk with my heart

I soon lost interest in him, but it wasn't long before I found his replacement. In Fifth Class, we had a new arrival at the school, and I was absolutely besotted with the boy. He was lovely and clean and perfect and the fact that he came from another school had my mind running ragged fabricating potential reasons for the transfer. Was he a bad boy who was expelled from his previous school for poor behaviour and looking to turn his life around? Had he entered into an FBI witness-protection programme after running afoul of a notorious gangster who stole a precious diamond? This is actually the plot to Mary-Kate and Ashley Olsen's *Our Lips Are Sealed*, so it was pretty unlikely that this was the case, but I got such a rush from inventing a backstory. Ultimately, it didn't matter why he ended up in my school, it just mattered that he was there. He was in the other class and our interactions were limited, so I had to settle for stolen glances in the yard at lunchtime. But one morning that all changed and I have Steve Jobs and the fact that my dad was a stickler for punctuality to thank for it.

My dad dropped me off at school quite early one morning when the gates were not even open. I stood outside listening to my iPod Mini, patiently awaiting the arrival of the caretaker, when I felt a presence approach me from behind. It was him and he was looking right at me. I felt see-through, like the clingfilm that was wrapped around the ham sandwiches in my lunchbox that my dad had prepared earlier that morning. I was defenceless. My heart was going ninety, and I was mortified because it was beating so brutally I was convinced he could hear it. He asked what song I was listening to. I couldn't even speak. All those years spent in Speech and Drama lessons after school, and I still couldn't utter a peep. The most I could muster was taking the iPod out of my pocket to show him the screen, revealing the track 'Don't Phunk With My Heart' by the Black Eyed Peas. How apt. Of his own accord, he took one of my earphones from my unsuspecting ear and popped it into his. The two of us now became one, connected by a tangled

Apple electroacoustic transducer, like a modern reinterpretation of *The Creation of Adam*. In that moment, nothing else mattered, and though it was a fleeting encounter, the memory of it would stay with me and confirm my suspicions: I liked boys. Whoops!

In secondary school, we started going to teen discos, and this was when the real trouble started. Hormones

were raging and pubescent lads turned into eager beavers on a mission to try and 'meet' or French kiss as many girls as they could (although I can assure you that there was nothing French about it). Venues such as Garryduff Sports Club, City Hall, the Savoy and Douglas GAA club hall were transformed into scenes mirroring a Netflix wildlife documentary, only short of some David Attenborough narration to seal the deal. Initially, I claimed that I had lost my 'frigit' status by telling the classic fib, 'I met someone on holidays last summer.' But this lie ran its course. I tried to ward off attention from girls by keeping to myself, but this proved difficult given my dance background, which meant I pulled focus on the floor when the 'Cha Cha Slide' came on. I really was doing the most with my Brylcreemed hair and the collar of my Jean Scene polo popped. To be fair, I did look cute. But any time I was asked, 'Will you meet my friend?' I would panic and say no. I just didn't want to. No offence, girls.

I kissed a boy and I liked it

Then I started drinking and, with the help of some Dutch courage, inhibitions receded and kissing girls became a bit easier. However, under the influence of alcohol, I also grew more eager to kiss a boy. But Cork is so small. I knew that if I was to ever be caught kissing a boy it would get back to one of my siblings and my 'dirty' little secret would be discovered. I used to lie awake at night in bed unable to sleep, consumed by troubled thoughts of my sexuality, wishing the gay away. Ultimately, I was in a privileged position in that I had openly gay relatives in my family, so I kind of knew that my parents weren't going to denounce me and throw me out of the home. But that didn't make me any less afraid. I knew something had to change. I was set on moving to London and wanted my friends and family to know who I really was before I left.

Coming out puts a queer person in a very vulnerable position. By sharing this personal part of ourselves we are giving the power to someone else to potentially reject us. It's also not a very accurate way of describing the experience as it suggests it's a singular act, a once-off that on completion never has to be repeated, whereas in reality this is not the case at all. It's recurring. Diana Ross is on repeat. We're constantly coming out. My best friend, Pádraig – who some of you may know as 'Pádraig from the podcast' – was one of the first people I told, and it was all very dramatic (which is a word that has never been used to describe anything either of us has ever done or been attached to).

Pádraig came to our primary school after he made his communion and, initially, I felt slightly threatened by his presence as he too was a theatre kid (I remembered his face from the *Feis Maitiú* circuit) – like he was coming for my gig. One of my first memories of him was when, during a class quiz, we were asked the name of Madonna's husband. We were about ten years old and most boys in the class probably didn't even know who Madonna was and wouldn't have been able to distinguish between Madonna and the school secretary if they were standing next to each other in a line-up. Without missing a beat, Pádraig whispered '*Guy Ritchie*' and I just remember thinking it was the funniest thing that he knew the answer.

Again, alcohol was the catalyst for courage when it came to coming out to Pádraig and I made sure that I was absolutely langers before I divulged anything. But no matter how many vodka rasas and Jaegerbombs I knocked back in Havana's on Hanover Street, I just couldn't bring myself to do it. When the club night came to an end, it was lashing rain so we decided to forgo the routine trip to Hillbilly's for a breast in a bun and jumped into a taxi together as we both lived in the same direction. I didn't want to come out in the car as I felt the driver would be listening, and did I mention Cork is very small and everyone knows everyone?

We pulled up outside Pádraig's house on the South Douglas Road and he threw me half the fare money and told me he'd give me a buzz the next day. I was raging that I had missed my opportunity, knowing that it would be another week before we would be out for a drink again, another week of sleepless nights with my secret. I asked the driver to hang on a second, jumped out of the taxi and followed Pádraig to his door. Again, reader, I'd like to remind you that it was lashing rain, like *ag doirteadh báistí*. Pathetic fallacy at its finest. Pádraig didn't know what was going on. We both stood in silence for a second, the shower now soaking us to the skin. He asked what was wrong and I told him, 'I'm gay.' Not even a second passed before he smiled and pulled me in for a hug. 'I knew it,' he said, and we were both laughing. And then he completely stole my thunder with his next remark, 'I think I am too,' followed by more laughing from the pair of us. The taxi man was beeping so we couldn't go into too much detail. Stop beeping, taxi man, we're both gay and having a moment! Another hug and I jumped in the taxi, beaming in the backseat the whole way home, overjoyed that me and my best friend had come out to each other. Or rather, that we'd both invited each other in. And that night, I slept soundly.

'How do you know you're gay?'

I was on a streak and wanted to keep the ball rolling, so I decided that my mam would be next. It was 31 December 2013 and I was headed to my friend's house to ring in the new year. I wanted to start 2014 off on a clean slate, with my family and friends knowing the truth – my one resolution. My mam offered to give me a lift, and I naively decided that the car journey would be a perfect time to tell her. My mistake. Her reaction probably would have been less extreme had Bertie Ahern popped his head out of the glove compartment and started playing the tune to 'Come on Eileen' on a kazoo. If you're LGBTQ+ and planning to come out to someone, do not do it while they're driving or operating heavy machinery. I just blurted it out when we were on our way down Donnybrook Hill and I'm lucky I'm alive to tell the tale. She was caught completely off-guard and swerved to pull over so that she could fully take in what I had just revealed to her. I always thought my mam knew. Apparently not. Eventually, she told me it was going to be okay, but she asked me not to tell my dad for a bit as he was off work for Christmas and she thought the vibes in the house would be awkward.

And maybe she was right. I didn't speak to my mam about it again until the Monday that my dad returned to work. She told me I should tell him that day because she didn't like keeping it secret from him. Eh, excuse me, lady, I wanted to tell him last week but you weren't about it! It got a bit heated and I started crying, and then I heard the front door open. It was my dad, and I didn't want him to see that I'd been crying, so I made a beeline for the biscuit cupboard, crouched down in front of the open door and buried my head among the Kimberleys and Bourbon Creams. My sister was with him and they immediately sensed that something was off. I stood up, red-cheeked, tears streaking down my face. My dad asked what was happening and I told him: 'I'm gay, Dad.' This was met with disbelief and dubiety and a whiff of hostility.

Then came the questions, my favourite being, 'How do you know you're gay?' I knew I had to tread carefully. I said I just knew. He asked what I liked about men and I asked him what he liked about women, a rebuttal I wholeheartedly regret. His response was, 'I like their shape.' Jesus Christ. Did we have to go into specifics? It was obvious he was overwhelmed, so he left the kitchen and went into the living room. He was off the fags at the time but that day he was cosplaying as Thomas the Tank Engine with the amount he smoked. My mam, my sister and myself sat in the kitchen crying. My mam said, 'Well, at least you told him.' And then, after all of about ten minutes to himself, my dad came back. He sat down with us at the table and then he broke down and started crying too. He said he was afraid. Afraid that life would probably be tougher for me because of my sexuality. He shared that, when he was growing up, he only knew of one gay person and they got a very hard time from everyone else and he didn't want his son to suffer the same fate. Eventually, we hugged and he told me he loved me and I think this resulted in more tears from my sister and mam. Everyone was bawling.

Car journeys with him were a bit awkward for a while, but pretty soon my dad learned that nothing had really changed. It was a bit of an anti-climax, to be honest. The world kept turning, time kept ticking and the big wheel on *Winning Streak* kept spinning on a Saturday night. In fact, my confession brought us closer. My dad became my biggest cheerleader and my best buddy. I think a lot of parents might have a similar reaction to my dad's upon learning of their child's sexuality. They're concerned for our safety, which is lovely, but really, it's not our responsibility to carry the burden of our parents' fears. We're going to be okay. We just need their support. And though telling someone you still love them sounds like a thoughtful sentiment, I feel like things have progressed and we can find better language. I mean, why wouldn't you still love me? Sure, am I not unreal? A nicer response would be, 'OMG, I'm gooped and gagged – are you top or bottom?' or a softer, more considered reply might be, 'I love you even more for trusting me and sharing this part of yourself with me.' Your child might be a bit mortified because in Ireland we struggle to hear things like this, but it will mean a lot to them. They haven't just come out to you – they've invited you in.

THINGS THAT ARE GAY THAT YOU DIDN'T KNOW WERE GAY

- o Sparkling water
- o Peace fingers in photos
- o Car-boot sales
- o Morning TV
- o Replying with memes
- o Naps
- o Maldon salt
- o Birkenstocks
- o CrossFit, especially since Kevin started going

- Sarah Michelle Gellar
- Libraries
- The food pyramid

- Photo dumps on Instagram
- Watching TV with subtitles
- Reading in general
- Any show with magic: *Charmed, Sabrina, The Worst Witch*, etc.
- Walking fast
- *Come Dine with Me*

- Getting in 10k steps a day
- Oat milk
- Brunch
- Clear iPhone cases
- Side tables
- Saucers – both the ones that hold your teacup and the UFO kind
- Footbridges
- Sarah Michelle Gellar's purple leather platform boots in *The Scooby-Doo Movie*
- Low-hanging lampshades
- Mixed media

o   Notebooks personalised with
    your initials
o   Anything that shimmers,
    including, but not limited to,
    diamanté, fish scales, tinfoil
o   'No junk mail' stickers

→ TWO ←

School and Education

'The more you read the more you'll know.'

PHIL TWOMEY

Kevin

A mump in the road

I know it sounds sad, and to be honest, it's mortifying to have to admit this, but I definitely peaked in school. I was that annoying child who used to get a cert at the end of the year for perfect attendance as I didn't want to miss a second of swotting. I used to play the Uno Reverse card with my mam and had to be the one to convince *her* that I wasn't that sick and was well enough to go to school when my symptoms suggested otherwise. The thought of missing out on valuable learning time used to send me into a state of shock, to the point where I felt I'd no other option but to drop out of the school choir, which ludicrously rehearsed on a Wednesday afternoon when I was meant to be in a maths lesson. The music teacher was undoubtedly disappointed by this decision, as I was one of the only boys who knew my crescendos from my diminuendos, and the only quavers the other lads had heard of were the cheesy Walkers crisps. I was definitely the Rachel Berry of the group. And I could read too.

I had a bit of a rocky start when it came to education. I was thrown multiple curveballs from the outset but I persevered undeterred. In playschool, a door came off its hinges and fell on my head and I thought it was curtains.

Realistically, I definitely could have put in a claim, but I'm not sure how seriously the courts would have taken a toddler in a suit, regardless of how cute I looked. But I did live to tell the tale and got a glass of MiWadi and some milk chocolate digestives out of it, so I suppose I didn't do too badly.

On my first day of primary school, I was beyond excited to get the ball rolling. Both of my brothers were already in big-boy school and I had serious FOMO, not knowing what they were getting up to while I was making the most of my afternoons with *The Morbegs*. But now it was my time. Catch you later, Molly and Rossa. My shoes were polished, my shirt was pressed and my *Space Jam* backpack was doing the most. When I set foot in the door, things felt correct and I was smiling from ear to ear as I waved my mam off to have tea and coffee with the other parents. I couldn't fathom why some children were screaming roaring when bidding their parents adieu. We were officially in big-boy school – why the tears? My stomach was in knots and my head felt a bit funny but I just thought it was the nerves and excitement for my new venture. Is this not what all big boys felt when starting big-boy school? Apparently not! Turns out I actually had the mumps. My first day was cut short and I had to be taken to the doctor, but at least I made a memorable first impression and the teacher would remember my name. Success!

It didn't take long to realise that I had a bit of a knack for the whole learning thing. The characters of Letterland became my besties (shout-out to my girlies Lucy Lamp Lady and Talking Tess – true allies) and learning my times tables was a bit of a breeze. One thing I did struggle with in those early years was mixing with my peers. I wasn't a fan of the high jinks that used to be commonplace in the yard at lunchtime, and I used to have trust issues when it came to sharing Legos because some boys were more excited about knocking down constructions than revelling in their craftsmanship. Chaos. One of my mam's favourite days of the year was the parent-teacher meeting, when she would be bombarded with compliments for her model-student child and quizzed on what her secrets were for raising such a studious son.

My time really came to shine in First Class when my teacher told us we would be putting on a production of *Aladdin*. Initially, I was cast as Aladdin's mam, Mrs Payalot. I didn't have that many lines but I was one of the few students in an all-boy class willing to play a woman. Red flag. One of the lines I had was, 'Come along, darling, I think I need a new Rolls-Royce. The one I have is at least a week old.' I didn't know what a Rolls-Royce was at the time but I evidently gave a confident and competent delivery in rehearsals, as the teacher used to laugh every time. The boy originally cast as Aladdin wasn't as adept as me in the art of line-learning and the cracks started to show. Two weeks before curtain-up, the boy was still a bit clueless. It was clear that something had to be done and, upon realising that I was already mouthing people's lines without looking at the script, my teacher knew that the right call was to hand the magic lamp over to me and, let me tell you, I was in my element. Me! The main character! It completely made sense with my fantasy.

As well as being my first introduction to performing and showcasing that I was a star, our First Class production of *Aladdin* revealed that I had a photographic memory – learning big chunks of writing off by heart was an easy feat for me. And the Irish education system completely catered to this way of learning.

TELEVISUAL DEEP CUTS

True icons are born, not made, and these deep cuts from our childhood are the reasons we rushed home after school and flew through our homework exercises in our *Busy at Maths* at record speed. We would spend as much time as possible sat in front of the telly watching our faves with a bottle of

Cadet and a Club Milk before we'd inevitably head out for a game of rounders or kerbs.

Bear in the Big Blue House

The fact that there was never a mention of a Mrs Bear and because the interior of the gaff was immaculate and would have had Dermot Bannon shaking, we have no choice but to assume that Bear is a big gay icon and lives it up at Berlin Bear week every summer in leather fetish wear. The song at the end of every episode is a Pride anthem, and can we also take a moment to talk about the *Bear in the Big Blue House* crisps? Honestly, we need to get a petition going to get them back on the supermarket shelves because they were divine.

Rossa from *The Morbegs*

Even though they looked a small bit petrifying, children around Ireland were glued to their tellies every time *The Morbegs* made an appearance. The fact that simple Irish was woven into the script of the show made the series even more iconic. One episode in particular sticks in my mind, where Rossa breaks down gender norms when he insists on wearing a pink skirt despite Molly's protestations that boys don't wear skirts and boys don't wear pink. Rossa walked so PJ could run. If Rossa was still around today, he would definitely be using they/them pronouns.

Totally Spies

Forget James Bond, these girlies were the real reason for my infatuation with fictional espionage as a child. The hair, the catsuits, the gadgets – they didn't miss a beat. When I was allowed to get my very first mobile phone in primary school and I insisted on it being the Motorola V220 flip phone it's because I was completely influenced by Clover, Sam and Alex, and even though nobody ever said so explicitly, I know that every boy in my class was jealous.

Bugs Bunny

Of all the cartoon characters going, few have mastered the art of gender-bending quite like our beloved Bugs Bunny. Bugs slipped in and out of drag seamlessly, often in an act of seduction to get out of a sticky situation with Elmer Fudd. Notably, pretending to be a woman was never just the butt of a joke. RuPaul himself even credits Bugs Bunny as one of his first introductions to drag.

Teletubbies

The Teletubbies have truly cemented their status as queer icons. When lined up together, they resemble a Pride flag, and all of their accessories are completely and utterly camp. Tinky Winky had a glam red purse for carrying his PrEP and Lost Mary Pineapple Ice vape. Dipsy had a stunning cow-print hat because fashion was his thing and he used to live for watching *Fashion Police* with Joan Rivers back in the day. Laa-Laa had an orange exercise ball that never left her side because she wanted to be the best in her aerobics class to impress the ridey instructor. Po had a scooter because she was always in a hurry (but always found the time to stop for an iced latte) and didn't want to get stuck behind the slow-walking straights.

SpongeBob

SpongeBob has always appealed to me because he has always unashamedly been his effeminate self. And though we already had suspicions about his sexuality, Nickelodeon cleared things up in 2020 when they announced that SpongeBob is, in fact, gay. When you think about it, most of the main characters in the show are pretty queer. Patrick definitely fancies SpongeBob, and the picture of him in the fishnet tights and thigh-high leather boots lives rent-free in my mind. Sandy is athletic and loves DIY, so is definitely a lesbian. Squidward is a textbook older grumpy gay neighbour and puts the bottom in Bikini Bottom.

Bagpuss

A striped, pink cat. Need I say more? Camp.

Kevin 11

Making the transition from primary
school to secondary is a scary step
for most people. For children
who feel different or other, the
advancement can be even more
intimidating. This is especially
true for queer kids. Going to an
all-boys secondary school as an
effeminate fella who likes acting
and dancing and detests any
form of roughhousing meant
I automatically had a target
on my back. The lisp didn't
do me any favours either. I
thought having two older brothers

already attending the school meant I would be off the hook
but, conversely, some of their friends partook in the teasing
and name-calling.

However, I didn't feel alone. I'm very grateful that my
best friend Pádraig clung to me like moss to a damp wall
and ended up accompanying me to the same secondary
school. Pádraig's earliest memory of me is seeing me in
the schoolyard at lunchtime pretending a traffic cone was a
microphone stand and singing 'Sound of the Underground'
with accompanying choreography. Even when I was that

young I had stunning taste in music. God, that song slaps. Myself and Pádraig started going to the same acting and dance classes together and would go to his house after school and compete against each other on *Singstar* on the PlayStation 2. His mam acted as our number-one hype girl. My go-to song was 'Round Round' by Sugababes; his was 'Superstar' by Jamelia. Again, immaculate music taste. So, we were always able to lean on each other and this made our time in school a little less daunting. We soon made friends with other lads who shared the same sensibilities and formed our tribe, which we aptly called the Sleepover Club. Or the SOC for short.

In the classroom, I continued to flourish. I loved languages and relished any opportunity to read aloud in English class to showcase my advanced literacy skills. But then again, all the gays were good at English. If you knew how to use a semicolon correctly when you were in school, you're gay now. Sorry, I don't make the rules. When it came to the Junior Cert, I got eleven A grades and was henceforth known as Kevin 11, a title I wore with pride. I was on the mental-health public-speaking team, head of the school bank, participated in the Young Scientist and played the lead in the Transition Year musical, among other endeavours. Looking back, I question whether my habit of overachieving had something to do with my sexuality. Was I constantly striving for perfection because I felt that my academic accolades made up for being gay? Perhaps I'm just a narcissist. The jury's out. Alexa, play 'Applause' by Lady Gaga.

I had so many interests and there were so many subjects that I was good at that I honestly didn't have a clue what to do after school. Filling out the CAO form had me sweating like a *Drag Race* queen who didn't know her lyrics for the lip-sync. The career-guidance counsellor didn't provide much insight either and I felt at a loss. The arts were what really got me excited, but I felt like if I was to go to drama school my years of grafting and grinding in school would be going to waste. So, I did my Leaving Cert, went on the obligatory Sixth Year holiday to Magaluf and dislocated my shoulder on the beach when attempting a front handspring in an effort to impress a girl (thank god for the EHIC) and ended up getting 580 points when the results came out in August. I got my first choice, which was Commerce International with French in UCC. And I actually ended up liking it. I got on well with the people in my class and loved attending French culture classes and felt like Elle Woods in my contract law lectures. But I also felt that something was missing.

I had joined the dance society at the beginning of the year, and one of the highlights from my time at UCC was going to Dublin for the dance inter-varsities. It was like a scene from *Bring It On*, so you can only imagine how obsessed I was. We came first place in the jazz category, and though I should have been buzzing on the bus home to Cork that evening I was actually left feeling a bit dejected, knowing that this annual competition was going to be my peak when it came to performing. I wasn't content with that. I decided I was going to drop out of UCC and audition for performing arts colleges in London. *Cue gasps*

London calling

My dad had an easier time accepting that I was gay than learning I was dropping out of college to move to England to train in the arts. It felt like a modern retelling of *Billy Elliot*. He thought I was throwing my life away and, to be honest, that crossed my mind too. But it was the best thing I ever did and I'm very proud of my 21-year-old self for making such a bold and brazen decision. When we're young it's so much easier to go with the tide instead of swimming against it. At times it was, of course, difficult and scary, and I wanted a sexy lifeguard to rescue me, but I just kept swimming. Studying at a musical theatre college can be quite an overwhelming experience. It's physically and mentally demanding and your peers also feel like your opponents and you're constantly comparing your ability to theirs. I made great friends at Masters Performing Arts and got on famously well with the teachers. Most of the male faculty were fabulous, debonair, older gay men whose camp references and witty remarks weren't lost on me. One time our jazz teacher sent my friend Zoe out of a dance class because she was wearing purple lipstick that he said looked horrendous. It sounds mean but afterwards we were all screaming laughing. The same Zoe has the most gorgeous curly hair and another member of the faculty said she should shave it all off for a more *edgy* look. Again, we were all screaming at the thought of Zoe with a buzz cut.

As with everywhere, the place had its fair share of wreck-heads. Typically, one would be able to avoid them, but you could be paired with them in a *pas de deux* or might have to sing through gritted teeth as you attempt a duet with them to 'Bad Idea' from *Waitress*. Just as well I'm a great actor. Even the students I liked I resented a small bit because some of them still lived at home and didn't have to work part-time jobs since they didn't have rent to pay. And the ones who didn't live at home still had the option of going home at the weekends while I had to make do with forehead FaceTimes with my mam and dad. I felt like I had sacrificed more than most people and also had more on the line given that I had dropped out of university to shoot my shot at stardom.

But I always felt like if I didn't give a career in the arts a go, I would regret it later in life. My thinking was that I could always go back to education but dancing was something I needed to do while I was young and my knees were still in relatively good nick. And this is how I justified it to people who were gobsmacked that I had ditched the textbooks for tap shoes.

Ultimately, I should have been happy to do it because I had a passion for it. I feel like in Ireland a career in the arts is still something that's frowned upon and isn't taken all that seriously. In England, you can study subjects like drama, dance and photography for GCSEs and A levels, but students don't have this luxury in Ireland. The fact that I was robbed of the opportunity to do a contemporary dance solo to 'Just Like a Pill' by P!nk is something I will never stop being bitter about. It would be great to see a shift in the system to encourage students who are interested in pursuing meaningful and fulfilling careers in the creative industries. These jobs are *real* jobs – and important jobs too. But please, please, please teach us how to do our own taxes. No shade to my accountant.

PJ

Define smart?

Unlike Kevin 11, I definitely wasn't the most studious boy in school. Nor was I excited to attend. In fact, I didn't want to go at all. I still remember my first and only day of nursery. Entering through a side door on Strawberry Hill (which I know sounds like a made-up location but is a real place), I clutched my mam's culottes before she suddenly abandoned me. I didn't go without a fight. I hung on to her trousers with all my might as the person in charge of this prison tried to lure me away with the promise of biscuits and games. I was taught the whole stranger-danger shtick from the moment I was born, and now all my mam was short of doing was kicking me into a white van. *Hypocrites*, I thought, *the lot of them*. Left to fend for myself in this foreign land, I tried to take it all in, questioning everything. Why was everything sticky? Were the other prisoners also abandoned by their mothers? Why is that one boy eating his shoe?

As I settled into life on the inside, I did what I needed to survive. I made an alliance with a girl I knew from the outside world, a neighbour two doors down from my old home. The warden told us we would be able to play games but we had to complete tasks first. We read books and were made to sing before I got the biscuits I was promised upon entering. We were then allowed some rec time in the playpen. It was like the Wild West in there and I don't think my social skills were developed enough to interact with anyone. After what seemed like an eternity, Mam came back and bailed me out. I described the hell I was subjected to and, as she always had a soft spot for me, her youngest, I never had to go back again. Instead, I had babysitters while my parents went to work. This suited me down to the ground because they were all lovely. But I was running out of time: when I turned four everyone around me was gearing me up for my move to big school and, unlike nursery, I couldn't drop out after one day.

The day came for me to start in Sunday's Well BNS (again, I know it sounds like a made-up place from a fairy tale, but I promise it's real). My mam took pictures of me on the disposable camera at home while my dad washed the car in the background. Then we all piled in and they drove me the three minutes up the road to my school. I can't remember my first day here as much as nursery, which I can only presume means it wasn't as traumatic. The one thing I do remember is two lads breaking the number seven in the number line, causing it to be off limits for the rest of the year. Looking back on it, maybe my junior infants teacher needed to address what caused her to hold a petty grudge for so long. Anyway, I was in the grips of the education system and there was no escaping now. I really didn't like learning things off by heart, especially spellings. It would always be really difficult for me to remember them when doing homework, and my dad shouting the letters I had forgotten at me would only cause my brain to get more confused. So, I devised a plan.

Every morning our teacher would go along the rows in our class and ask us individually how to spell a word from our spelling homework. I don't know how I did it, but I worked out that if I asked to go to the toilet roughly three people before me and stayed in there until the teacher passed me, she would forget to come back to me and I wouldn't have to spell anything. This worked for about a week before she stopped letting me go to the toilet, so I had to get creative. I'd write out the spellings the night before and, like a glam secret agent straight out of *Oceans 11*, hide the tiny piece of paper on my chair in between my legs. Thank god I had 20/20 vision. I'd try to work out what sequence she was asking the words in and glance at the paper a few people before me to see the word I was most likely to be asked, and the majority of the time it worked. Could I have put all that energy into learning my spellings? Yes. But are people just smart in different ways? Also yes.

My struggle with reading and writing persisted throughout my schooling. I was part of this special trial group in my school where we were hooked up to a laptop and had to read and spell things on screen and the program would repeat it all back to us in a recording of our own voice. You'd think being singled out like this would have been embarrassing and made me subject to bullying but it weirdly just felt special, and it was my first time using a laptop, so that was exciting. My primary-school teachers threw around the word 'dyslexia' a bit, but I was never tested and it's still something I wish had happened because I would have been able to bring the laptop home, enabling me to go on the internet and visit the most sought-after website of our time: www.amandaplease.com

Pick me, choose me, love me

So, I was successfully conning my way through primary school, but one thing I couldn't do was con my way into the popular group. I partook in the high jinks that Kev avoided in hopes that it would earn me points with the popular lads. This is when the people-pleasing began. At the time, I obviously didn't deep it as much but, looking back, I was thirsty for external validation. I was always with the popular kids but never really in the *inner* circle. This was never more obvious than when we all used to hang around in an estate called Hillcrest after school. One of the lads had converted his shed into a snooker room. It was giving money, which equalled popularity. From Fourth to Sixth Class we all hung out in the shed. Prank-calling people, sneaking girls in, smoking fags we robbed from our mams, that sort of thing. I would do anything to be part of the group, but it never seemed to be enough. I was so thirsty for them to be my friend. Looking back on it now, I'm mortified.

One day, the main bitch suggested we play a game of Tip the Can: a game where one person is 'on' then everyone separates and hides, trying to avoid being caught while also freeing the people who have been captured. Surely everyone knows Tip the Can, right? This would be deemed childish if anyone else suggested it, but because the popular guy did, we were all on board. I was asked to be 'on' first, so I counted as everyone hid. I searched for a bit and found nobody until I saw all of them running around the corner as a group. I chased after them but they kept running away from me and laughing. It wasn't until my friend Jamie – the only true friend I had in the group – found me that I knew what was really going on. He explained that the main bitch made the game up so that everyone could run away from me because I was being annoying.

Excuse me? Annoying? I was barely talking. Anyway, I started crying uncontrollably and ran home to mourn what just happened. I could barely breathe and my throat felt worse than when I smoked that fag in the shed. This, in theory, should have been a character-defining moment for me. Like when the protagonist in a tween Disney film renounces the Populars, finds true friends, gets the guy and undergoes some form of makeover montage in the process. In my case, however, I went back the next day with loads of packs of chewing gum to try to bribe them into liking me. It didn't really work but at least their breath smelled nicer as they bullied me. Even typing this now I'm realising I struggle with the whole people-pleasing thing to this day. It sticks with you, girlies.

Cruising Pana

It was when I got to secondary school that I cemented a group of stunning individuals that became my core group of friends. After the drama that was the entrance exam, and touring a private school I couldn't afford and didn't get into anyway, I ended up going to the local school that all the lads went to. It was chaos in there. During my first week, I saw a first year get his head dunked in the toilet, something I thought only happened in the aforementioned Disney films. Another guy got a locker door smashed in his face, and I saw a boy no older than 14 smoking a joint on our break. It was a rough school, and some of the teachers were trying their best to clean it up but, Jesus, they definitely had their work cut out for them.

Jordan, Dylan, Jamie, Mossy, Dean and I were all besties. Now, we were like something out of *The Inbetweeners* but it just worked. Jamie, Mossy and I all went to the same school, and as soon as Jamie started to drive at 16, we'd pick Dylan up after school and drive around the town, or 'cruise Pana' as we used to say. Cruising Pana was basically when you drive around Patrick's Street, one of the main streets in Cork, just for a nose. Dean is my nephew and would join us sometimes. Before you think this was a *Baby's Day Out* situation, where we'd be spinning around with a literal child, Dean and I are 26 days apart in age so we've always said we're more like brothers, but I always make sure that he doesn't forget that I'm the eldest. You must respect your elders, regardless of the time between births. I learned loads in those 26 days. In school, I'd have to have my guard up, and watch what I said and how I acted so as to not be targeted, but around these lads I could let that drop and just be myself. It was refreshing to be able to exhale.

The boys in my year had so much potential and were really smart, but you could see that a lot of what was happening in their home life was bleeding into the classroom. The poor teachers in our school went through it. I lost count of how many times one ran out of the room crying. Our geography teacher would get into such a rage that I thought the vein in his head was going to explode like Mount Vesuvius over Pompeii. Which was, ironically, what the poor fella was trying to teach us about. I felt so bad for those teachers. I remember one lady asking the class to stop throwing paper balls. As she stood in front of us, tears in her eyes, she delivered one last plea before a paper ball from the back of the classroom came and bonked her on the head causing the entire class to erupt in laughter and for her to run out of the room and never return. I think she actually retired to Spain, which seems lovely, but I felt so guilty for not saying anything.

Cheeky little pup

During Transition Year, which most of my class skipped because it wasn't mandatory, I think something flipped in me. While a lot of people left after Third Year to start apprenticeships and the majority went straight to Fifth Year, myself and a handful of the lads spent Fourth Year having a skit and deciding what we wanted to do with our lives. There must have been something in the water, because when we went into Fifth Year we were all determined to do well in the Leaving Cert, and there were some amazing teachers going above and beyond to help us achieve that. I was so grateful that they saw the potential in us and wanted to nurture it. Teaching is so difficult and I think it takes a certain type of icon to be a good one. Imagine having to put up with cheeky teenagers, and not only resisting the urge to tell them to fuck off but also wanting to help them. Saints. There were definitely some of those in my school, but there were also teachers who I don't think even wanted to be there. In it for the summer hols, am I right, girlies? They'd phone in each lesson, not caring if we did the work or not. Primary school spelling-cheater PJ would have loved this type of teacher, but I'd grown up since and now, as I wanted to better myself, I became an awful moan.

I spent more time in the principal's office during Fifth and Sixth Year than I did my whole schooling life, but it was never for high jinks, it was for 'talking back'. It used to boil my blood when they said that. One teacher had completely given up on teaching us the syllabus, to the point where we used to teach ourselves after school. During his class, we would do the same exercise over and over again and I'd argue and fight with him every time. A 'cheeky little pup' was the title that the teacher bestowed upon me. The gag is that the fab teachers knew I was right, so when they saw me outside the principal's office they'd just laugh or roll their eyes in sympathy. I broke my dad's heart, though, because he'd always be called in and after a few meetings couldn't fathom why I couldn't just keep my mouth shut and respect my elders. When I opened my mouth to answer his question, he'd snap and be like, 'There you go again, la!' – so yes, I was an intolerable teenager, but in my defence a lot of the things I got in trouble for saying I stand by to this day. I just don't get in trouble now because I'm an adult and people take my opinions seriously. Well, most of the time.

Maybe you agree with me on standing up to lazy teachers. Like, obviously, if we felt like we weren't getting the education we deserved, we should have had the right to speak up about it. The other area I got into trouble for, though, may divide people: I was suspended around three times for not abiding by the hair- and dress-code. I just couldn't wrap my head around how not wearing an earring was going to make me better at school. The first time I got suspended was because I got a haircut that was too short. It was a skin fade and when I was sent to the principal's office, he told me that the reason dress-codes exist is to train us for the real world. He said that nobody would hire me with a skin fade. Number one, that statement has a pong of classism off it, and two, he didn't know what I wanted to be. Anyway, I told him I wanted to join the army after school and they all have hair like this, to which he called me cheeky and rang my dad. He was right, I was such a little shit.

I was so excited to finish secondary school. I was so done with academics and just wanted to be free. Plot twist: in between arguments and suspensions I managed to get Student of the Year twice and got the second-highest Leaving

Cert results in my year, losing out to a guy called Kenneth, but I didn't mind as he studied so hard and I think he's like a doctor now or something.

I've since gone back to that school to give a talk about pursuing a career in the arts, and I finally got to thank the amazing teachers who supported me back then. It's great to see that they're continuing to make the school better, but I wouldn't go back to education if you paid me. I just hate academia. I feel trapped and like it's not made to cater for me. I even tried to go back and study marketing at a university in London at one point, but lasted a term before dropping out. I found that I learn more when I'm doing. Learning as I go, with whatever haircut I want, wearing whatever I want. It's a privilege I'm well aware of and I'm grateful I get to do that every day. So, in short: ABOLISH TRADITIONAL EDUCATION! No, I'm only joking. Unless ...

READ FOR FILTH

The library is open, girlies, and we've compiled a list of all our favourite LGBTQ+ books that we think you should check out once you've finished reading *The I'm Grand Mamual*. There's a good mix in there: some will make you laugh, others will make you cry, but most importantly, all of them will make you look like you're giving off big main-character energy if you choose to read them in a café or on public transport. Remember, reading is fundamental – and hot.

o **Straight Jacket** – Matthew Todd

o **Fun Home** – Alison Bechdel

o **Detransition, Baby** – Torrey Peters

o **At Swim, Two Boys** – Jamie O'Neill

o **A Dutiful Boy** – Mohsin Zaidi

o **Call Me by Your Name** – André Aciman

o **Shuggie Bain** – Douglas Stuart

o **Dancer from the Dance** – Andrew Holleran

o **On Earth We're Briefly Gorgeous** – Ocean Vuong

o **Swimming in the Dark** – Tomasz Jedrowski

→ THREE ←

Styling and Self-Expression

'Sure, who'll be looking at you anyway?'

NUALA KIRBY

PJ

A blade-two buzzkill

'Sure, who'll be looking at you anyway' is a saying my mam and I never really agreed on. Growing up in the small town of Cork, I felt like everyone was looking at me. Some of this was because I was trying to keep my homosexuality a secret from everyone, but also it's because Irish people are generally just awfully nosy. My mam isn't too much of a gossip, but she's a loving woman and people tend to open up when they're around her, so by default, I got to hear all the tea every time she met a friend on the street. A two-second hello could quickly turn into our own personal two-hour news report about the whole parish.

* News broadcast music plays*

Hello there, I'm a random woman your mam bumped into on North Main Street. Here are the headlines: Sally's dyed her hair since Seán left. It's shocking. Poor Joe's died, not d-y-e-d like Sal, he's passed, sure God love him. Also, Grace has lost all the weight from doing Slimming World in the parochial hall.

And in news just in, I've just clocked that your son PJ is a bit fruity.

More on that in my next report. Good evening.'

As the parish news anchor disappeared to do her next broadcast, I would always have the same thought. One I still believe to this day: people judge you the minute they see you. Before you open your mouth, people have made assumptions about you based on how you do your hair, what you're wearing, your weight, if you have any physical disabilities, the list goes on.

I didn't always believe this, and there was a point in my childhood where I was blissfully unaware of being noticed. It was in Senior Infants. Every lunchtime, John, Ricky and I used to go to the corner of the room by the sink where they dropped off the milk cartons, and play salon. We would give every hairdresser in Cork a run for their money as we took our tracksuit tops and tied them around our heads, like a person would do with a towel when they got out of the shower. Suddenly, three lads with blade-two buzz cuts now had glamorous up-dos that we could pretend to style. We were in our element. It was so fun, so freeing and it felt so right to play with my new friends. That is, until some of the other boys in the class began to make fun of us. They called us sissies and I think they even used the term 'gay', which was mad because I'm sure we were literally six years old. Anyway, I panicked and chopped off my new hair, putting my jumper back to the way that was deemed acceptable by the majority of the class.

I distanced myself from John and Ricky, as the mixture of freedom and shame I felt when I was around them was

too much for baby me to handle. We were given uniforms so that we were all the same and we wouldn't stand out, but it seems even that didn't stop me. I seemed like a lost cause and needed to learn the rules fast. Branded tracksuits were cool, especially when paired with Nike TNs, pink was for girls, as was anything glittery, and wearing a football jersey was the easiest way to fit in. Well, that was until I was asked about the team whose jersey I was wearing and needed to learn some facts about Man United that I could reel off.

I became good at blending in and knowing what trends to follow. The girls had to fall in line too. You were nobody without jelly shoes and a Bang on the Door lunchbox. Coming into our teens, the boys graduated to check shirts from The Jean Scene while the girls got their hands on ra-ra skirts and stilettos they couldn't walk in. We were fitting into the little gender roles that were set out for us, but I was so jealous of the rules the girls were assigned. I wanted to wear sparkles and cute prints and to dip-dye my hair, but the rules were the rules, and if you broke them, you were othered. This didn't stop me from finding hacks. As a teen, I'd tie my check shirt around my waist so it felt like a skirt to me but to the world I was still 'dressing like a man' – another phrase I never quite agreed with. How men dress changes so much. Who could keep up? Like, you're telling me Julius Caesar could wear a stunning floor-length gown but I can't wear pink or I'll be called gay? It's actually hilarious.

Yes way, Jose

Moving to London and coming out in my twenties is when I truly started to experiment with fashion. It's like being gay suddenly freed me from these gender norms and the anonymity of the big smoke let me experiment away from nosy neighbours that might bump into my mam on North Main Street. Oxford Street became my runway and I was obsessed with the models I was walking it with. There were powerful women in power suits strutting past drag queens in full glam and nobody batted an eye. In this city, my mam's words rang true. I could wear what I wanted and do my hair how I liked – sure, who'll be looking at me anyway? But I still felt shackled to the old rules. I'd explore what different versions of myself looked like in London, but once I stepped off the Ryanair flight at Cork Airport, I'd regress. I'd pack some clothes from London that I'd be nervous to wear back home. When I plucked up the courage to wear them, the town would have a crick in their neck from staring, so I held back. That is until I met the fashion icon himself, Mr Jose Galang.

After I met my now-fiancé, the fear of being seen as 'different' began to dissipate. We both love fashion, and early into our relationship, we would gag over a designer's new drop or what we found in vintage stores, pushing each other to take risks, and protecting one another when we did. It's easier to walk the street with your head held high when you have someone cheering you on as you do so. The difference in the way I dressed in London compared to Ireland was now minimal.

The rules still existed, but I didn't care anymore. I felt powerful, and locals getting cricks in their necks were no longer my concern. I want to say that clothes became genderless, but then they always have been. We as a society just decided who should wear certain items. Now I shop in both female and male sections, depending on what type of mood I'm in. I can pair a shirt and tie with a skirt and boots without thinking I'm making some sort of statement.

Do it for the baby gays

Back in London, Kev and I spurred each other on too. We were living in Stratford behind the Old Stratford Mall. It was there before they refurbished all of Stratford for the Olympics back in 2012, so everything around it was brand new but the mall felt frozen in time. It's like the government focused so much on the Westfield mall next door that they just left this one to its own devices, like a once-manicured garden that's been allowed to grow wild.

I was obsessed with it. There were stall owners screaming at the top of their voices, shoplifters being chased by security, fully grown men bombing through the place on electric scooters, and breakdancers blaring music and practising their moves on the sticky floor. A great place to people-watch, but not a place to model your new queer fashion. We'd usually walk through the mall to get to the Tube unless we were serving a look that might draw attention – then we would take the long route to the station to avoid it.

One Pride, though, with the help of some Dutch courage, Kev and I decided, *No, we're going to strut through this mall and leave its patrons shaking.* Now, we were terrified as we entered the chaos in crop tops and some sort of mesh but we pushed through and got to the Tube. We were weak for ourselves because of this little win, hyping each other up by saying things like, 'Do it for the baby gays,' and 'We're not going to mute our queerness.' To this day, Kev says I'm addicted to that phrase.

I'm definitely shedding these gender norms as I become more comfortable with myself but obviously they're still there. Take hair, for example. How is it that when a woman wants to cut and dye her hair she basically needs to remortgage the house, when a guy can pop to a barber's with a €50 note and have change left over? It's insane how, just like clothes, we treat hairstyles differently depending on whose head it's attached to. This divide was never more clear than when I was getting my hair cut in a barber's in Spitalfields in London. I was midway through my skin fade and we were making mindless barbershop talk. I was feeling a bit uneasy, not because of anything he was doing, but just because that's what the barbershop does to me. When I was less confident in myself, I would deepen my voice, and not necessarily go back into the closet, but I would hold on to its door handle for comfort, dodging any question that would force me to have to come out to the very straight man cutting my hair. As we were talking, a woman in her twenties walked in and asked for a cut. She had short hair similar to mine, so I was shocked when the barber said he couldn't cut her hair as they only cut men's hair. I mean, what a load of bollox. She wasn't asking him to put in nine-inch extensions, just wanted a back and sides like me. She accepted her fate and left before I could even object. I was fuming. My mindless chat turned into more of an investigation. I was giving big Olivia-Benson-from-*Law-and-Order* energy and I was a member of the elite squad. Dun, dun. The interrogation uncovered that the owner of the shop had told his employees to say the place was only for men: a traditional barber's. Yock, like. When I asked what he would do if a non-binary person who he thinks looks more female came in, he didn't have an answer. I left and never went back.

Aren't we all big rides?

It's time to gaslight ourselves into forgetting the rules. I think that once you stop paying attention to the rules, you truly unlock a type of transformative power. When you wear something that makes you feel confident, it has a huge impact on your mental health. Why do you think we all like to get dressed up just to go get our silly little coffees? Making the effort and styling yourself the way you want to is liberating. I know I'm coming across like one of the *Queer Eye* presenters, but dressing in a way that makes you feel confident is freeing. I'm not saying every young fella needs to wear a dress – just wear whatever makes you feel comfortable. Dress for yourself, not somebody else's gaze. Confidence is the sexiest thing in the world. If you feel hot, you'll look hot, and you'll only get there by feeling comfortable with yourself. People in Ireland have an awful habit of putting themselves down. More often than not, when someone is complimented on their outfit, it's met with disagreement, followed by the cost and location of where the garment was purchased. The Irish, myself included, are terrified to love themselves. We don't want to be seen as having notions, but, sure, what's wrong with that? Aren't we all big rides?

Some people reading this might be perfectly happy with how they look, but for those who want to step out of their comfort zone style-wise, this is what helped me: As I get ready, I think of what character I want to be that day. Styling yourself is just like playing dress-up when you were younger. Do I want to give sexy secretary vibes, do I want to dress like a Bratz Boyz doll or do I want to serve a cute wholesome look? They're all different characters that are tied to my different moods. I try not to take it too seriously and if I am ever afraid to wear something I ask myself why. It's literally just clothes.

I've realised that all along I've been reading that saying wrong: 'Sure, who'll be looking at you anyway?' I thought it meant, 'It doesn't matter what I look like, because nobody will be looking at me anyway,' but now I see it more as, 'Who is the person looking at me, anyway?' Are they judging me because of the way I look, or are they judging me because they're not happy within themselves? Now if I get nervous about someone judging me for an outfit I want to wear, I ask myself, *Who is this imaginary person that will judge me? Why will they judge me and does it matter?* I've come to the conclusion that it's none of my business what people think of me (and yes, that's another mammy phrase we should add to the book).

UNDERSTANDING UNDERWEAR

I know we just said that what you wear doesn't matter, but from personal experiences we have developed our own underwear hypothesis. We believe that you can gain a greater understanding of someone based on the underwear they opt for. A vague litmus test for someone's character, if you will. Please see our findings below.

Boxer

Typically worn by dads, lads and discreet tops who hit you up on Grindr looking for a late-night shag but won't kiss you because 'that's definitely gay, bro'. A boxer-wearer is

still a bit of a schoolboy at heart and enjoys life's simple pleasures. They're likely to have owned the same pair of boxers for a few years, but who cares? Boxers are considered a bit retro chic these days and have come back into fashion, and we love when they're coupled with baggy jeans and you can see the plaid waistband peeking up towards the torso.

Boxer brief

Calvin Klein is solely responsible for making boxer briefs the cultural crowd-pleaser they are today. The boxer-brief-wearer knows what he wants and isn't afraid to go and get it. Classy and confident but can also be a bit of a gobshite. Definitely one to break up with you over text as opposed to meeting face to face. Has money invested in various cryptocurrencies and loves to tell people about it.

Brief

Okay, you're a whore, we get it. It's also likely that you're European. You're body confident and so you should be. Typically the underwear of choice for the Men at

Play gang, so it definitely gets our seal of approval. The pouch for your private parts leaves nothing to the imagination, which is ideal because you love to show off. You take your time when you're getting ready in the changing rooms and we're not mad about it.

Thong

In the words of Sisqó, 'Let me see that thong ... That thong, th-thong, thong, thong.' We're so happy that lads have started to embrace the thong in all its skimpy glory. The thong-wearer is the crazy one of the group and is always up for a party. You worship the ground Charli XCX walks on. You thrive in the summer and love your trips to Sitges or Gran Can, where you can lie on the beach, drink some sangria and flirt with the other *guapo chicos* who are there to have a good time.

Jockstrap

You love getting the arse cheeks out. It just feels comfier. One thing you love more than wearing your jockstrap is telling people that you're wearing one. This sometimes culminates in you sharing a picture of you in your jockstrap to your close friends on Instagram. And sure, why not? You never skip leg day and your bum is your fave feature. You tell people you're vers but really you're a die-hard bottom, and we take our hats off to you.

Kevin

My Graham Norton Moment

Saturday nights always felt special when I was growing up. After a week of work and worrying about mortgages and cholesterol and other things grown-ups fret about, my mam and dad would meet with friends and head down to their local in Douglas for a few drinks. In my dad's case, it was never an alcoholic drink as he was a lifelong pioneer, dismantling the Irish stereotype one glass of ginger ale at a time, whilst my mam opted for a gin and tonic. Icon. My nan would come over to mind myself and my sister for the evening, and I absolutely adored her so I relished her arrival. Time with my Nana May was sacred. We'd watch *Criminal Minds* together and drink tea and stay up late – I was in my element.

My mam would always call me up to her room while she was getting ready. I used to love the smell that came from her blow-drying her hair and applying her signature Carolina Herrera 212 scent. She'd always ask the same question, 'Does this look okay on me?' and I would always tell her she looked beautiful. This, however, never sufficed, and she would produce other options and I'd be encouraged to weigh in and pick out my favourite. But she never really asked anyone else in the family to give their thoughts on her rigouts. Just me. My sister Sarah found rotting. I was acutely aware that only my opinion seemed to matter to my mam, which was slightly unnerving. She was singling me out for my sensibility but also encouraging it. What made me more qualified than my other family members to give my two cents? Was I … a fashionista?

When I was growing up, the gay men on TV were always fashionistas. Fully developed narrative arcs for gay characters were non-existent, but, boy, did they know how to put a look together! The roles were one-dimensional; the sassy hairdresser or the bitchy best friend who helped with a makeover at one point or another. If their exaggerated mannerisms didn't give them away, then their outfits almost always did. I was drawn to these characters because I saw a semblance of myself in them and they were a deviation from the norm. They looked fun, even though they lacked depth and were often played by straight actors. (Which I'm not a fan of, unless it's Eric Stonestreet's portrayal of Cam in *Modern Family*. He plays a gay man better than any gay man I know, and should be studied.) These characters provided insight into people I wouldn't have otherwise known existed, and that was exciting. But most of the characters were fictional and typically American, so it all still seemed far away from me.

Enter Graham Norton, stage left, in a beautiful, bejewelled blazer. My ring-of-keys moment.

My first introduction to Graham Norton was when he played Father Noel Furlong on *Father Ted*, which resulted in me re-enacting his iconic rendition of 'Bohemian Rhapsody' for anyone who would listen for months after. (*'LET ME GO!'*) When he started hosting his own show, I loved catching glimpses of it, even though a lot of the content probably went over my head. He was camp, colourful and – to top things off – he was from Cork! A person from the rebel county who gained notoriety for reasons other than sporting success or involvement in the War of Independence. I didn't know such people existed! He was characterised by his ostentatious sartorial style. It was flashy and flamboyant, unlike the clothes worn by other men his age on television. The way he dressed felt special. I wanted to feel special.

A Judas Kiss from A Jacket

When I was in First Year, my mam bought me a brown Regatta jacket. The first time I wore it to school I was told it was gay. Well, it was news to me! Forget aussieBums and leather harnesses, the true gay garment that trumps all other articles of clothing is the unassuming brown Regatta jacket. I should have known! I felt tricked. Was my mam not aware that it was gay when she bought it from Debenhams? Had she not done her due diligence and checked for the jacket in the faggy fashion directory? The jacket that had kept me warm in the winter had betrayed me. But I didn't care. I continued to wear the jacket, because if Graham Norton could sport sequins and sparkles on prime-time TV on a Friday night, then I could muster the courage to sport my brown Regatta jacket to school.

It wasn't the first time I had learned that a certain item of clothing was, in fact, gay. Pádraig once stopped wearing a pair of suede Puma shoes his mam brought him back from Lanzarote because he was told they were gay. Another boy in my class was forced to get signed out of school early on a non-uniform day because he had chosen to wear tracksuit pants that had popper buttons up the side, which were obviously gay. (Poppers!)

The American retailer GAP experienced an unprecedented drop in sales in Ireland in the early millennium when a mastermind acronym analyser in our school came to the dramatic realisation that the brand in fact stood for 'Gay And Proud'. How were we so dumb?

I continued to try not to care what people thought about my clothes, but as I got older, in the absence of any suggestion of a girlfriend and amidst a growing fondness for Lady Gaga and salt lamps, attempts to ward off people's suspicions of my sexuality started proving difficult. I tried throwing people off the scent by getting my left ear pierced (left ear = hetero; right ear = homo; both ears = bi), but this only bought me a few weeks at best. I started dressing down in an effort to not stand out. I wore a lot of the clothes that had once belonged to my brothers, and for the first time, I started to blend in. Even on holidays, away from the prying eyes of my peers, I was guilty of committing the ultimate act of compliance as a heterosexual Irish man abroad by wearing a Cork GAA jersey. This was chaos, considering my only involvement with the sport was when the Cork team won the All-Ireland and were paying a visit to our school, so I got my mam to buy me a sliotar to have signed just so I could get up close to the sexy players. Mad that they call him Seán Óg when he's a big hunk of a man.

But when I moved to London, this all changed. I didn't know anyone, so I could wear what I wanted without the fear of judgement. A clean slate. At dance college, I was surrounded by other gay lads who weren't afraid to push the boat out, and this gave me the confidence to do the same. And then came the rite of passage that most people who move to London in their twenties go through: I discovered the vintage shops of Brick Lane and bought myself an oversized shirt and a purple Adidas windbreaker and thought I looked the absolute tits. I didn't have much disposable income in my early years in London, so a lot of my clothes came from charity shops and smelled like wet dog and sweat, but at least they suited the cool aspiring-dancer aesthetic adopted by most of my friends. In hindsight, I was really just conforming again, but I was happy because I was trying something new. My dad, however, wasn't so happy.

Someone could have died in that

Any time I was due to fly back to Cork, my dad would make it his mission to be the one to collect me from the airport. His excitement at the arrival of his prodigal son would be marred slightly upon noticing my choice of ensemble bought on a recent spree in Oxfam or the British Heart Foundation. As I ambled into arrivals dragging my trusty suitcase (purchased in Salou ten years prior) behind me, I'd spot my dad's moustached visage and watch his expression shift from joy to 'What the heck has that gobshite got on him?' He would hug me and kiss me and insist on carrying my suitcase, but before we would even make it out to the car he would comment on my outfit. Despite my protestations that all the cool kids got their clothes in charity shops, he couldn't wrap his head around the idea of me willingly wearing things that once belonged to strangers. He would always say, 'Someone could have died in that, god rest them,' which even now still makes me scream. On one occasion, he brought me straight from the airport to Mahon Point Shopping Centre and gave me €50 to buy a new outfit, because he didn't want people to think we were struggling for money. What a man.

Shortly after graduating, PJ and I moved into a house together in East London, and we made it our mission to go to the coolest queer nights in the city. I learned very quickly that jeans and a nice top weren't going to cut it at these particular soirées, where fabric and inhibitions were scarce and gender-based clothing norms went out the window. Everyone looked sexy and knew they looked sexy, and it all seemed effortless. I had to step my bussy up! Initially, it was nerve-racking, especially when we were travelling to and from the club. We would forgo the Tube and pay the extra few quid for an Uber to avoid the looks and laughs from people on the Central Line who were jealous that they didn't look as hot as us. And though it was scary, the fact that myself and PJ had each other when we were dressed outrageously was comforting and made me feel a bit safer. The boy is six foot four and is built like a brick shithouse, so even if a fella had an issue with the way we were dressed, they typically never tried their chances. My own personal bodyguard in a skirt. I'm really grateful I had PJ by my side.

The anonymity of London definitely helped when we went out dressed like raging homosexuals. An impromptu encounter with an uncle and having to explain why I was wearing leather trousers and a mesh wrestling singlet with my nipple piercing visible underneath wasn't likely to happen. But on one occasion, myself and PJ travelled back to Cork for Pride, and obviously it was my intention to serve a look. I wanted to wear a green mesh crop top with a black beret, but getting ready in my childhood bedroom with my parents downstairs made me shrink back into myself. I was mortified about what my dad would think if I were to come down looking like a moody French cucumber. I felt like I had taken two steps forward and three steps back, and for a minute I contemplated changing outfits and wearing something a little more reserved and ordinary. But visibility is important, particularly at Pride. I was thinking of the young queer people who would be out in Cork that day and remembered the impact that seeing Graham Norton in a fussy and fancy blazer on TV had on me when I was young, so I decided to bite the bullet. Do it for the kids! And my dad didn't really bat an eyelid. In fact, I think he liked the outfit. If I remember correctly, I believe he said, 'You better slay the house down, boots work mama … The Saturdays 'Greatest Hits Megamix' … Yasss bitch, okurrrrr …' when I came downstairs. Or something to that effect.

Second-hand and stunning

Nowadays I still buy a lot of my bits in charity or vintage shops. She's eco-conscious, girlies! We all know by now that fast fashion is having a seriously negative impact on the world. Not at all cute! Along with its supply chain, it's the third-largest polluting industry after food and construction. We all love a bargain and are lured by the cheap price tags and next-day delivery options, but somebody, somewhere, along the chain is paying. I know it's not easy or realistic for everyone to only buy pre-loved items or clothes from ethical slow-fashion brands, but I do think it's important for us to re-evaluate the relationship we have with our clothes.

Shop savvy and buy bits that you can mix and match with other pieces instead of something that you're only going to wear once on a night out and never look at again once you've gotten the pic for the 'gram. Learn how to take proper care of your clothes: fellow Cork girlie and camp icon Laura de Barra has a stunning book called *Garment Goddess*, which tells you everything you need to know about minding, mending and maintaining everything in your wardrobe, and I would definitely recommend getting yourself a copy. Making a move to more sustainable practices when it comes to fashion puts pressure on the industry to start changing and ultimately will result in a more positive outcome for the planet and for the people making the clothes who are being exploited for profit. And our girlie Greta Thunberg will be happier, too.

I still don't think I have a fully realised sense of what my own personal style is. It's always evolving and I'm constantly reinventing myself to keep the girls on their toes, just like Madonna (only I've skipped the chaotic *Madame X* era). But isn't that the fun of it? Every morning, when I wake up and open my wardrobe, a new opportunity to wear what I want and showcase a different side of myself awaits.

In Ireland, the phrase 'Sure, they love themselves' has long been regarded as one of the most scathing insults to be uttered about a person. You're dead right, Susan – I love myself, and I hope someday you can learn to love yourself too! There's no crime in confidence and feeling good about yourself and how you look. And if dressing a certain way makes you feel more confident, then fecking go for it, because, like Nuala says, 'Sure, who'd be looking at you, anyway?'

'ALEXA, PLAY "HAIR" BY LADY GAGA ...'

In the words of the streetwise ginger orphan Annie, 'You're never fully dressed without a fade.' I am at my most powerful when I've come out of the barber's looking all brand new with a bazzer. It's the final step in making me feel like an absolute ride and when you see me coming with my fresh fade, you better lock up your sons and husbands because I'm ready to wreak havoc. But getting your hair cut can be a nerve-racking experience. As a queer person, the anxiety is heightened because barbershops are typically quite masculine spaces where conversations about football matches, cars and liking steaks and smoking cigars are rife. You're in foreign territory, a timid flamingo abandoned in the lion's den hoping to escape unscathed. (Did you know that the collective term for a group of flamingos is a flamboyance? How camp!)

Regardless of how comfortable you are in your sexuality, it's easy to slip back into old habits and assume the role of an actor once more, nodding and smiling as if you know what your barber is talking about when they mention unfamiliar terms like 'transfer window' and 'craft beer'. In my own experience, I would recommend getting an explicit mention of your homosexuality into the conversation as soon as possible. Rip off the plaster to reveal your rainbow in all its technicolour glory. Maybe when showing your barber a picture of the hairstyle you'd like, slip in the fact that you'd love to shag the fella in the photo or something subtle like that. It's not easy, but you owe it to yourself to not have to entertain a boring hetty tête-à-tête when all you want is to have your gruaig looking gorgeous. And you might be surprised. My current barber is an absolute lad but is such a sweetheart and loves hearing all my gay gossip and is so tender when he touches my head it makes me want to sob. And it's cheaper than therapy, too, girlies.

→ FOUR ←

Love and Relationships

'See how they treat the waiter at the restaurant.'

PHIL TWOMEY

Kevin

St Patrick's Blessing

I remember the first time I kissed a boy. It happened on Paddy's Day on Patrick's Street in Cork and his name was Pat. The last part isn't true, but could you imagine if it was? Let's just use Pat as a pseudonym for now, because I don't want to mortify the boy. I was 20 years young and it was obviously after a few drinks, given the day that was in it, because I'm very patriotic and St Patrick's Day is when we celebrate the snakes being banished by getting absolutely locked and listening to 'C'est La Vie' by B*witched. Even though I was out at the time, I was still slightly traumatised about the prospect of kissing another boy in public, but I threw caution to the wind because I was so desperate to have my first experience and to try something most of my friends had been doing for years. It was what St Patrick would have wanted.

I was also slightly nervous in case I wasn't a fan of the whole gay kissing thing, because I'd already told everyone that I liked boys, despite having never so much as sniffed somebody's son before in my life. What if I didn't like it? Obviously, I loved it, and though there weren't any fireworks or a flashmob to Carly Rae Jepsen's 'This Kiss', like the movies would have us think, it felt right. And I was weak for myself. I knew from then on that kissing boys was something I was going to do a lot of and, girlies, you best believe I was ready to make up for lost time.

Back then, I used to like any boy who showed me a bit of interest. For so long I had lusted after lads who were off limits; either because they were straight or because they were fictional characters in a TV show (basically every single one of the actors in *Desperate Housewives*; Mike Delfino if you're reading this, I would let you hit me over the head with one of your wrenches and I would probably say thank you, ya big flah). And having someone fancying me felt so new and exciting and almost taboo. The first time I saw two men kissing was in Christina Aguilera's 'Beautiful' music video and, though I was mesmerised by it, I forced myself to look away because it just felt wrong. I grew up thinking my attraction to men was shameful, so once I was at a place where I was comfortable with my sexuality, I became an eager beaver and wanted a fella.

And there were a few fellas. There was the lifeguard I met in Savoy nightclub who took me surfing and I was mortified because I looked like a drowned rat for the entirety of the date. There was the bodybuilder from Essex who took me to a Toby Carvery on our first date, and I was shook at how much roast beef he was able to horse into himself. There was the doctor from Bradford who was gluten-, dairy- and nut-intolerant, and I bought him flowers on our second date. There was Pedro from Gran Canaria, who didn't understand

a word of English but, my god, was he fecking gorgeous. There was the boy who worked in B&Q who was very tall and kind and still slides into my DMs when I put up a fire pic on Instagram. And then there's my ex, who was the first boy I loved and the first time I introduced a boy to my mam and, realistically, I'm still not over him and he's so handsome and maybe I should text him …

BREAK-UP DO'S AND DON'TS

Even when they are amicable, break-ups are a tough thing to go through. It's giving grief! Confusion, anger and simply feeling a bit lost are all part of the process and though time is a healer of all things, these are some extra tips you can follow when you're picking up the pieces and trying to move on.

DON'T post about it on social media

Reposting random cryptic quotes to your story on Instagram isn't that cute and ultimately nobody really cares. Though in the same breath, I kind of love it for the drama? Okay, so maybe do so sparingly.

DO spend time apart

Even if you're looking to remain friends after a split, it's still probably a healthy idea to spend a significant amount of time away from each other without any contact so that you both can heal. If you are looking to remain friends, remember most friends don't shag each other after a couple of glasses of wine on a Saturday night.

DON'T romanticise things too much

If you look back through your camera roll, you're likely to be bombarded with photos of you both looking cute AF together and having a great time (so many brunches!) and pretty soon you'll end up forgetting why you split up in the first place. I'm not saying you should delete all the pictures; it's nice to have the memories, but remember we really only ever tend to document the fun times.

DO look as hot as poss at all times

It's a slightly terrifying thought but you can bump into your ex at any given moment, so do yourself a favour and alleviate the stress by ensuring that you are the sexiest version of yourself every time you set foot out your front door. Even if you're just taking out the bins, slip into something slinky, pop the stilettos on and give your hair a toss.

DON'T stalk them on social media

In fact, unfollow them. You don't need the constant reminders that they are getting by just fine without you, and checking whose photos they're liking and commenting on is going to send you spiralling. Archive the WhatsApp chat as well to avoid the temptations of a drunken 'miss you' text.

DO take some time off the apps
There's the temptation to get stuck into things straight away and get back on the boy-bandwagon, but give yourself a chance to decompress and reevaluate what you want. A rebound shag is of course fine, but just be open with the person that that's all you're looking for.

DO find healthy ways to occupy your new time
Chances are you used to spend a substantial amount of time with the person you broke up with and now you have spare time on your hands, and you don't want to be left twiddling your thumbs and contemplating sending them a message. Prioritise yourself. Start a new skin-care routine, pop the AirPods in and head for a walk or maybe even learn a new skill, like voodoo-doll-making.

Catholic guilt

Though things didn't work out with any of the lads above, I'm still grateful that I met them. Okay, maybe not the fella from Essex, he was a bit of an eejit, but with the others I definitely had a lot of fun and, in some cases, maybe even learned something about myself. Speaking of fun, there are also the boys whose names I don't know, one-off wonders I hooked up with when the urge came calling, brought together by fate in the night. And by fate, I mean Grindr *insert Grindr message alert tone here*. I used to get so anxious when it came to casual sex, to the point where my body would start shaking uncontrollably once I'd confirmed a *rendezvous* with a gentleman friend. (*Rendezvous* is French for ride, by the way.) Again, shame probably played a part in this anxiety, and it also reared its head afterwards when I would be left feeling like I had done something wrong, despite having a fun time with another consenting adult. The Catholic guilt thing really did have me by the neck for quite some time and took a lot of unlearning on my part. But we're getting there.

HOW TO HOOK UP SAFELY

Some tips to bear in mind to ensure a hook-up is as nice as it can be:

o   If you're meeting someone at their place, let a friend know the address and the person's name. And make sure they don't live with their parents. Or if they do, make sure their parents are out and not returning for quite some time. This is more common in Ireland but sometimes happens in London too and obviously there's nothing wrong with living with your parents (housing crisis, girlies) but it's just not worth the stress of having to tiptoe around the gaff like a character from *Scooby-Doo* from the moment you set foot in the door. Also, nothing kills the mood quite like catching a glimpse of a family photo on the mantlepiece when you're in the middle of doing bits.

o   PJ used to know when I had a boy over because I would move some of the plants from other parts of the gaff into my bedroom. This really adds to the aesthetic.

o   Have music playing from the moment they arrive to help with the atmosphere. Frank Ocean is always a good go-to. Just make sure your Spotify isn't set to shuffle. I once had the prologue from *Little Shop of Horrors* come on mid hook-up and it was a bit of a jump-scare. (Yes, I know all the words.)

o   Ask for multiple photos to make sure you're a match
    for each other. If someone sends pictures that are
    giving pixelated *Crimecall* CCTV footage, or if they
    have a chaotic filter on all their pics, ask for clearer
    ones. Better still, ask if you can video-call them before
    meeting.

o   If, like me, you're big on hygiene, communicate this to
    the person you're meeting. It sounds pretty obvious, but
    some people are a bit clueless.

o   Say no to Deliveroo. Okay, this one needs some
    explaining. I once had a fella at mine, who upon arrival
    mentioned that he was starving and asked if he
    could order KFC to the gaff, and to this day I'm still
    traumatised by the sight of the greasy fried-chicken
    stains on my sheets.

o   Set clear expectations with the person that you're
    meeting to ensure you're after the same vibe. Have a
    conversation with them, and agree on parameters so
    that you both feel as comfortable as possible.

o   Have your first meeting in a public place.

o   Be self-sufficient. Bring your own condoms, lube,
    poppers, etc. Don't rely on the other person to have
    these. Maybe even bring your own candle in case his
    room is smelly.

o   When you meet someone, don't deepen your
    voice because you think it makes you sound more

masculine. Your voice is yours and it's already sexy.
Especially if you're Irish. Even more so if you're from
Cork. Sorry, I don't make the rules.

o   Get tested regularly and have open communication
    with the person you're meeting about your testing
    history.

o   Always have a bottle of San Pellegrino in the fridge so
    that if your guest wants a glass of water, you can come
    out with 'Still or sparkling?' That's camp.

o   Have some gay literature (see p. 70) on a desk nearby
    so he thinks, *Wow! Hot* and *clever! This boy's a catch!*

o   Remember, you can change your mind. Consent is
    key when it comes to sex and can be withdrawn at
    any time at your discretion. Check in periodically with
    your partner(s) to make sure they are comfortable with
    what's happening. Pay attention to body language
    and ask, 'Is this okay?' Make sure everyone involved
    consents before escalating or changing activities.

The greatest gift

Another reason why I experienced so much anxiety about sex
was because I simply didn't learn about it. There was little or
no education in schools on LGBTQ+ sex and sexual health.
Realistically, in Ireland the entire sex-ed curriculum needs an
overhaul. When we were in Sixth Class someone who wasn't
a nun but was definitely weak for God and Jesus came to give

us 'the talk'. She described sex as something that happened exclusively between a man and a woman, and we were told it was the 'greatest gift' to give someone when you're in love. Personally, I'd prefer something more useful like a Dyson hoover or maybe some Le Creuset cast-iron cookware, but each to their own, I guess. We were then shown a diagram of a vagina. One of the lads in our class fainted and the rest of us were inconsolable. I left feeling even more confused than I had been before; at the age of twelve I was still questioning whether I was having wet dreams or wetting the bed.

In secondary school there was a longer digression that covered STIs and contraception but still no mention of gay bum sex. Sad times. I thought that film and TV might fill in the blanks, but when I was a teenager there still weren't that many depictions of queer relationships on screen. The only one that really jumps out at me is Willow and Tara's romance in *Buffy*, which was kind of iconic, to be fair. But again, not much gay bum sex. This meant that we had to learn as we went, which wasn't exactly the best way of going about things. We relied on friends or sexual partners with more experience than us to show us the ropes. And in the absence of friends and lovers we looked to porn, which often paints an unrealistic portrayal of sex. None of those football players in the locker room after practice are having gay sex for the first time, despite what the video description might say. Trust me.

LET'S TALK ABOUT SEX

In an alternate universe, one where the Catholic Church didn't have the schools of Ireland in a chokehold, I would rewrite the SPHE syllabus in secondary schools to include the following nuggets of knowledge:

o Douching tutorial.

o Body positivity: loving yourself before making love to someone else.

o U=U: undetectable means untransmittable. HIV-positive people who are on effective treatment and have an undetectable viral load cannot pass on the virus to sexual partners.

o PrEP: oral medication taken by HIV-negative people to protect themselves from contracting HIV.

o The importance of consent: communication can be verbal or non-verbal with body language. Even if you consent to a sexual act, you can change your mind before the act begins or at any time before it ends.

o Masturbation is a laugh and isn't just for lads.

o Some people have no interest in sex, and this is normal.

o Your vagina doesn't look weird. Every body is different.

o Sending nudes: not sharing someone else's nudes without consent.

Single but sleeping soundly

I don't really think I have a type when it comes to fellas, and I don't have all that many prerequisites for potential partners. I'd like for them to be funny, but under no circumstances are they to be funnier than I am. Could you imagine how awful that would be? I would literally have no personality. I'd like for them to be an early riser but not so early that they make me feel like a lazy bitch for waking up later than them on the regular. Ideally, they wouldn't make noise or move in their sleep. Better still, they would sleep standing up. Or would that be too scary if I was to witness it in the middle of the night? Their income would sustain the two of us so I would never have to work and could focus on more important things like going to yoga and drinking Bloody Marys with the girlies on weekdays. Novelty socks are an absolute no-no, and if I ever see them run up the stairs on all fours it's game over. And most importantly, they have to be kind – that's something I couldn't compromise on. My mam says, 'See how they treat the waiter at the restaurant.' I don't want them to be too nice to the waiter, though – that'll just make me jealous.

Social media can sometimes have us comparing ourselves to others and we can be left feeling like our lives don't measure up to the ones lived by the people we see online. By now, though, we should be aware that a lot of Instagram consists of carefully curated and contrived posts by people who realistically probably do eat Coco Pops for breakfast but only document the açai bowls. Yet despite having an awareness of the disingenuous nature of the platform, we still compare.

But it's not just the influencers doing yoga courses in Bali or the *Love Island* huns who are releasing new clothing lines off the backs of exploited and underpaid workers who are doing it. Sometimes it's our friends. It happens to me every Sunday when I see an Instagram story of a friend who has had a similar day to my own, only they're doing everything I did that day with a fella by their side. And though I didn't feel lonely during the day, I do in that moment. But I try to brush it off. And then I think about the platonic relationships in my life and feel better, because those friendships are so important. They're fulfilling and feel like home. Also, I hate sharing the bed with someone, so, although I'm single, I always get a stunning night's sleep and that keeps me looking young. I know that the right person will come around at the right time, and until then I'm going to enjoy my uninterrupted eight hours of slumber.

A CRAVING FOR SNACKS

The following is a list of lads we were absolutely weak for when we were growing up but could never tell anyone about because we were in the closet. They're the boys we longed for and lusted after, and had things been different, we definitely would have had magazine pull-outs of the boys showcased on the walls of our teenage bedrooms.

Zack from *Saved by the Bell*: The original himbo king, Zack was a true snack. This show really had it all and Zack had us wishing we could trade places with his love interest Kelly Kapowski and walk the corridors of Bayside High with Zack on our arm.

Ricky Martin: 'She'll make you take your clothes off and go dancing in the rain.' Oh Ricky, I really wish you would. G'wan. Go for it. I won't look, I swear.

Hanson Brothers: Literally couldn't decide which of the three were cuter. So why not date all three of them? Don't fight over me, boys.

Lil' Bow Wow: He first came on our radar when he starred in *Moesha* and we all sobbed when he was shot in the movie *Like Mike*. The fact that he called himself 'Lil' Bow Wow' just made him extra adorable.

Brock from *Pokemon*: We wanted to be Ash but wanted to get with Brock. A bronzed Adonis who never really opened his eyes, so he was super mysterious, which is super hot.

Spike and Angel from *Buffy*: Sure, we watched *Buffy* because it was so iconic to see Sarah Michelle Gellar, a badass female protagonist, be fearless in her pursuit of protecting Sunnydale from vampires and other demons, but we also watched it for the ridey lads. Spike and Angel are the reasons we love a bad boy and they had us wanting to risk it all. Special mention to Riley from the end of Season 4, who was also gorgeous.

Quizmaster from *Quizone*: If you didn't watch *Quizone* growing up, are you even Irish? We all wanted to be on the show because it looked like the biggest laugh ever but also in the hopes of getting close to the absolute daddy that was the Quizmaster, who had our minds racing in that referee uniform. It was giving role-play.

Tyson Beckford: Hearing the song 'Toxic' made me gay. Seeing Tyson Beckford shirtless on the back of a motorbike made me even gayer. They just don't make music videos like they used to in those days. Red-haired, leather-catsuit-clad Britney traversing through an obstacle of lasers and the iconic trolley trot in the cerulean blue air-hostess uniform have also made lasting impressions for obvious reasons. But the crimes I would have committed to be on the back of that motorbike.

WWE wrestlers: A huge cause of contention in our household growing up was who would gain ownership of the remote control on a Saturday morning. If my oldest brother got the remote then I begrudgingly would have to watch WWE, which I despised. But it wasn't all despair. Seeing the sweaty wrestlers lift each other up and throw each other around the gaff used to elicit unthinkable urges in me, the type you'd have to go to confession for. Most of them were unreal, but special mentions to Chris Jericho, Randy Orton and John Cena – love you, girlies.

Duffman from *The Simpsons*: Matt Groening knew exactly what he was doing when he created the musclebound,

Lycra-clad god that is Duffman. *The Simpsons* is an exceptional show and Duffman made the viewing experience even more worthwhile.

Shawn and Marlon Wayans: Every time I had a sleepover at my friend's house, I would insist on us watching *White Chicks* because 1) it's hilarious and 2) it also starred these sexy brothers. Special mention to Terry Crews who is also a flah and had us learning all the lyrics to 'A Thousand Miles'.

Harvey Kinkle: *Sabrina* was peak '90s television. The opening credits were outstanding, the spells and special effects were next level, and the boys were immaculate, particularly Harvey Kinkle. When he let his hair grow long I honestly had a pain in my chest because I fancied him so much. Also, Hilda and Zelda were gay icons and the cat, Salem, was camp as Christmas.

Maxxie from *Skins*: *Skins* shook all of our adolescent minds to the core, but I was more focused on one episode where the bleach-blond Maxxie gets out of bed naked and you could see his bare backside. The pause button was worn out that year.

Robbie Williams: Robbie was a naughty boy and, my god, did he cause a lot of mischief and confusion when he released the video for 'Rock DJ' in which he stripped down to his undies. Things got a bit dark when he started tearing off his skin and we were slightly traumatised, but it was still kind of stunning.

Taylor Lautner: There was no question about it. We were #TeamJacob and wouldn't have minded if he imprinted on us.

Sam from *Glee*: Similar vibes to Maxxie from *Skins*. Bleach-blond twunk energy. Fun fact: his stage name is Chord Overstreet, which gives me the ick.

David Kawena from *Lilo and Stitch*: I know he's a fictional cartoon character but he nearly had me taking up surfing so we had something in common. Also, honourable mention to Cobra Bubbles, who's a daddy.

Joaquin from *The Cheetah Girls 2*: He could sing, he could dance, and he made Dorinda shut up about being adopted for five minutes.

PJ

My shotgun wedding

The first time I said 'I love you' in a romantic way was to Jessica O'Connor on our wedding day. It was a simple outdoor ceremony with only two witnesses and the priest. After exchanging vows and a peck on the lips, we had the afters in my kitchen, where we served MiWadi and purple Cadbury Snacks, because we were seven and my sister didn't have the budget for anything else. Of course, this wasn't an actual wedding. My older sister Lindsey and Jessica's older sister Michelle woke up one day and must have been sick of playing with their Baby Borns because they decided to have a pretend wedding. After enlisting the help of my neighbour Sarah, who played the role of priest, we busied ourselves with the prep, and before I knew it, I was hitched. Even though this wedding was a sham, I wanted it to be special – I mean, I even wrote the vows that I said during the ceremony.

I've always been a hopeless romantic. Growing up, I'd watch romcoms and my heart would nearly explode out of my chest when the guy raced through the airport to stop the girl from getting on the plane. On Valentine's Day, I'd write cards to whatever girl was in the vicinity. Of course my wife, Jessica, got one, but the next year it was my friend Claudia, then Sarah. It didn't matter who was getting the card – it was just an excuse to pour my heart into a card. Looking back, this is kind of fuckboy behaviour. I'd slip the anonymous card through their letter box, which nine times out of ten, contained a limerick-style poem I'd written and some crêpe paper hearts that would fall out when the card was opened. Honestly, the whole thing was high camp, and I think that's why I loved it so much.

Jessica, coincidentally, was the first person I ever properly kissed. We were all hanging out in the woods and learning how to kiss 'like they do in the movies', which to us basically meant attacking each other's mouths with our tongues. I would now like to issue a written formal apology for the way I kissed Jessica on that day. I think she said my tongue was like a washing machine, which doesn't sound too pleasant. You know me, though, girlies – I'm a hard worker, so I put in the practice. We'd go to teenage discos covered in a combo of Lynx Africa and Joop to see how many girls we could kiss while Maniac 2000 played softly in the background. I never did well at the discos. I wasn't much of a looker, and I also think they could just sense I was a raging homosexual. One night, however, I was on fire. Everyone wanted a piece. Maybe it was because I could do the rave or maybe because I had a fab glow-stick necklace on, but the girls couldn't get enough.

I think I was after kissing nine girls – or 'meeting' as we would say – when my friend asked me to ask a girl to ask her

friend to meet him. I strutted over to the group of girls like how I'd imagine John Travolta would in *Saturday Night Fever*. A dated reference, I know, but I will allow it. I was so in the zone that I didn't notice the puddle of spilled Coke on the ground. I flew up into the air, landing flat on my back. The music cut as the whole disco gasped before erupting in laughter. They all then started to throw rubbish at me and call me a faggot. Only messing, of course, that didn't happen, but it felt like it did. I peeled myself off the floor as the girls giggled in their group before returning to my friends who were also laughing. And with that, my winning streak at the discos came to an end.

Costa Del Soulmates

As I grew older, I began to question if love was even real. I know that sounds bleak, but all around me relatives and friends' parents were breaking up and getting divorced. Also, the couples that were together just seemed to hate spending time with one another. 'I'd better get home before the ball and chain kills me,' my dad's friend would say after they came back from the pub. Now, I'm sorry, but I would never want to be referred to as a physical restraint device popularised by the British Empire in the seventeenth century.

The shining example I had for love was my mam and dad – honestly, I feel so lucky to have parents who loved each other so openly when a lot of my friends' parents were separated or not on good terms. I remember one year we all went on a big family holiday to the Costa Del Sol. We'd usually do a trip somewhere in Ireland, but my mam had just got early retirement so we went on a big sun holiday. They were like two teenagers, the pair of them, kissing by the pool, messing on the beach and dancing around the restaurant while Lindsey and I buried our heads because we were mortified. Well, Lindsey more so than me. She was older, so approaching teen-angst territory, and I was just copying her because she was my older sister. I secretly loved that they were gallivanting. It proved to me that real love was out there, and I wanted to find it.

My hoe era

As an out-and-proud gay man in London during my early twenties, I always valued dates over hook-ups. Although my track record says otherwise, I promise that I did want to go on more dates, but when I first dipped my toes into the gay scene it seemed like a quick ride was higher on my suitors' priority list than a nice dinner. Of course I obliged. I'm not a prude, after all, and if we weren't going to have a romcom-style love affair I might as well get my bit. So, there were fewer dinner dates and movies in my early twenties and more sending face pics and late-night Ubers home. It was fun, but I always craved a deeper connection. I wanted to find someone, my other half. I had a few situationships and one short-term boyfriend but I never fell head over heels for them. It was as if the *idea* of having a boyfriend was more appealing than actually having one, so this led to me being a bit of a fuckboy, where I'd lead people on and then kind of bunk them. Sorry, lads, I was young, dumb and full of … confusing feelings.

Jump forward to 2015, and I was over fellas. *All men are trash, so I'm just focusing on myself and my career from now on*, I told myself. I'd sucked off too many frogs that didn't turn into princes, so I was channelling my love into my other passion: dance. I went back to Dublin for a dance intensive, as there were going to be international choreographers there I wanted to learn from. I was walking into the studio, determined to make my mark, when I was completely blindsided. As I watched a group of dancers rehearse, I couldn't stop looking at this one fella. I'd seen Jose years before at a workshop and we followed each other on Instagram. Every time he'd pop up on my feed, I'd get a little tingle in my stomach, but now that I was in the room with him it was like that tingle was a small fire that someone just poured petrol on. He was physically gorgeous, of course, but it was more than that. The energy that was radiating from him was something I'd never felt before. It made me feel calm and safe while it also sent my heart racing and gave me butterflies. If someone asked me before this moment if I believed in love at first sight, I would have laughed in their face, but here I was falling in love with this person; so maybe not at first sight, but definitely second or third. I'm actually mortified by how in awe of him I was. As he laughed with his friend it was like he was moving in slow motion, for feck's sake. Impressing the choreographers was off the table. I had a new goal.

Chicken liver lovin'

I used all of my skills to try to get his attention. In class, I'd pretend not to know what was going on, so I could ask him. I made friends with all of his friends, so we could sit together at lunch. Things were progressing nicely, but I was running out of time. Soon the intensive would be over and I'd have to go back to London and what if Jose met some dumb twink before I got the chance to make him fall in love with me? I needed to resort to teenage disco tactics. I told Jose's friend Kerrie that I liked him, and she delivered the message on the last day of the intensive. We all went to Nando's and obviously news of the budding romance spread because all the dancers were Team Posé (they didn't give us that celeb couple name, but they should have). We all ordered and he got chicken liver – *She's different*, I thought, *not like other gays*. As the night drew to a close, I had to go for it. After awkwardly asking for his number, we parted ways to start what became six months of courting.

We'd text each other constantly and made trips to Ireland and London to see each other. We shared our first kiss on my childhood bed in Cork, which was a bit of a full-circle moment for me. The bed that I used to lay awake in at night, feeling guilty for my homosexual tendencies, was now being used as a platform to kiss this ride of a fella. When Jose visited me in London for Valentine's Day I asked him to be my fella in another awkward, cringe moment. I suppose that, because a lot of queer people spend their teenage years in the closet, we almost go through another adolescence when we come out later in life; we still need to experience our romantic firsts, causing us to act like awkward teens in our twenties. He said yes. And so began a long-distance relationship of six years.

GOING THE DISTANCE: LONG-DISTANCE RELATIONSHIP TIPS AND TRICKS

When I tell people we were long distance for six years, their jaws drop before asking, 'How the fuck did you manage that?' Well, firstly, the plan obviously wasn't to be long distance for so long, but it just ended up being like that. Many factors were at play: I was just getting going with my career in London and Jose with his in Dublin, getting a UK work visa for Jose was a pain and also there was a global pandemic thrown in there at some point. Between the highs and lows here are things that helped us not fall apart:

Schedule virtual date nights

Just because you aren't in the same place doesn't mean you shouldn't designate time to do things together. For example, we love to cook, so what we would do is pick the same recipe and then cook it together on Zoom. With Jose in Dublin and me in London we'd go through all the steps of the recipe and then eat it over candlelight as if we were together, while watching the same film. It would make our virtual calls feel more special and less mandatory.

Have a reunion date in the calendar

Always have a date booked in the calendar where you are going to be physically together. This becomes a crutch that you can lean on when you feel like it's all pointless. Every day that passes is a day closer to that date.

Keep it sexy

Send nudes, sexts, hot videos, whatever you're into, but you need to try to keep things spicy between meet-ups. It's exciting for both people – the person taking the bits and the person receiving them.

Park your stubbornness

It's too easy to stay odd and give someone the silent treatment when you live in different countries. Instead of holding a grudge, you need to try to talk openly and honestly when you're annoyed at one another.

Surprise each other

Do something the other person isn't expecting. Send a letter or a care package. Bring them on a surprise trip. Make them a custom playlist. It's less about what you're actually doing and more about doing an unprompted act of love for the other person. It makes them feel special.

Can't pour from an empty cup, girlies!

Although the long-distance period of our relationship went on for longer than expected, it's given us skills as individuals and as a couple that I don't think I would have learned otherwise. Growing up, I always thought about couples as two halves that complete each other and always romanticised that notion; you need each other and that's why you're together. But throughout the years I realised that we're both two whole individuals who choose to be with each other, which I think is a hundred times more romantic.

Because of the long distance, we unlearned the co-dependent habits we'd picked up early on in our relationship. Jose will have a different experience of this, but I learned that I was such a romantic growing up because I was searching for people to love me so it would validate me. Coming from that mentality only leads to disappointment, in my experience. As wanky as it sounds, I really did need to learn how to love myself and stand on my own before I could offer some love to Jose. You can't pour from an empty cup, and I think that you can't love someone else if you have not built up that love within yourself first. I also learned the value of non-romantic relationships. Friends are just as important as lovers. Your partner can't be everything for you, and there are some things that friends are just better at than your partner. I've found I need to work on my friendships in a similar way to how I work on my romantic relationship.

Now don't get me wrong, Jose has helped me love and believe in myself in ways that I'll always be grateful for, but it's in choosing to love each other every day that gives us power as a couple. We have been changing and growing as people in the seven years that we have been together. I had to learn how to love many different versions of Jose and he had to do the same for me. The main principles that I will be taking into our next chapter as we prepare for our wedding are that I'll never take Jose for granted, I'll make sure to communicate when I don't think something is working and, above all, I'll choose to love him, the big flah from the dance intensive.

→ FIVE ←

Moving Away and Making Money

'We've never died
a winter yet.'

NUALA KIRBY

PJ

So, I'm standing in Sainsbury's as that alarm goes off, you know the one when your card declines. As it bellows from the self-checkout machine, I say to myself, *What sick fuck thought that it would help the situation if everyone in the supermarket knows about it when your card is declined?* As this self-checkout basically calls me poor I frantically try to find a staff member to help me void some of the shopping so that my card will go through. This is a risky game as I also couldn't afford to top up my data this month, so I can't check my online banking to see what my balance is. The dance begins, the unimpressed manager uses his key card to void some luxury items such as avocado and sourdough. I enter my pin and it declines again. We repeat this routine until I only have the bare essentials: rice, tofu (I was in my vegan era at the time) and wine. I think it was my third attempt when I realised that our electricity bill or something must have come out of my account and I had reached my overdraft limit and this transaction was never going to go through. I needed to plan my escape. I was so mortified and wasn't thinking straight, and I don't know why my brain went there, but I honestly was going to fake an epileptic fit to save face. When the manager said that it's probably an issue with my bank I thought that was a much easier excuse to go with instead of me dropping to the floor and poorly and offensively re-enacting a fit I saw a girl from the Youth Club have when I was 15. I just agreed with the manager about the bank and ran out the gap.

PJ, there's people that are dying

It was my first year in London. I had moved from Cork to follow my dreams of being a dancer. Things weren't working out and I was broke and kind of sad to be honest. The 'eating the leftover food from the table you just cleared in your waiting job' kind of broke, which nowadays makes me an anti-food-waste sustainable icon but back then I was just starving on my twelve-hour shift. My mam was so good and helped me where she could, but London is ridiculously expensive. So expensive that I was looking at any way I could make money. I even looked into selling my used underwear once, but you'd max get like, £50 for them. Once I factored in buying the underwear and the postage and packaging, it was more effort than it was worth.

Early on in London, a lot of the time on my days off I'd have no money to do anything so I just watched the Netflix I was signed into – I don't know who was paying for it but it definitely wasn't me. I was kind of half-depressed and half-hungry most of the time, but I was also like, *PJ, calm down, you're grand, people are literally dying and homeless. Stop feeling sorry for yourself.* Then I was mad at myself for not letting myself feel sad. Everyone's struggle is their own and all that. Let's just say we weren't in a good place, girlies. Then I was thinking, *How in god's name did my parents raise a whole family and always have food in the gaff and clothes on our backs.* Growing up, I never worried about money or wanted for anything. That's not to say we never had money troubles, but my mam would always know we could get through anything. 'We've never died a winter yet,' she would say every time we got a big utility bill or some unexpected repairs needed to be paid for. She knew we would come out the other end. In those early days in London, facing the first big-boy problems, I thought of my mam's stunning outlook. *I'll be grand*, I thought, *we've never died a winter yet.*

This, I suppose, is what happens to most people when they move away from home. We've jumped out of the nest and need to learn how to fly but, Jesus, you definitely hit a few branches on the way down, don't you? When you move out to live your independent-woman fantasy, the first branch you hit is housemates. Unless your parents are filthy rich, you need to move in with people to cover the rent. It's a gamble. If you move in with friends, you risk hating each other; if you move in with strangers, you risk them being an Ed Sheeran superfan and nobody wants 'Shape of You' blaring when you poach your eggs in the morning.

THE EIGHT TYPES OF HOUSEMATES

Housemates: can't live with them, can't afford to live without them. Only messing, some of your cohabitants can become your besties for life and others may land you in prison for manslaughter. To determine which one is which, we've broken them up into eight archetypes.

THE SOUND ONE

This is the dream housemate. You both get on, might cook dinners and go to events together, but respect each other's boundaries. You definitely have a side-WhatsApp where you gossip about everything that's going on in the main group chat.

How to deal:

No need. You're probably going to become great friends, but definitely schedule a brunch and bitch every now and again to air your frustrations about the painful housemate.

THE MAMMY

Let's be honest, the house would fall apart without this person. They're the only person that truly knows how to do adult things, such as properly using a washing machine and knowing how tenants' rights work. They're usually the eldest sibling in their family.

How to deal:

They may like to look after everyone but they need looking after too. Take some tasks off their hands from time to time.

THE PARTY GIRL

You've a love/hate relationship with this person. As they're an extrovert to the highest degree, you have a great time with them at a party but they also never stop inviting people over, turning your home into the local parish hall seven nights a week.

How to deal:

Chat to them about why it's sometimes annoying to come home to other people in the house when your social battery is on the floor and you just want to relax.

THE RECLUSE

You know they exist because their name is on the lease, but if they went missing you'd find it hard to describe them to the Gardaí because you've only seen their face once as they scurried to the bathroom. An unproblematic housemate but may also be a serial killer.

How to deal:
Knock on the door every 4–6 weeks and check for a pulse.

THE CLEAN FREAK

Cleaning rotas and passive-aggressive sticky notes on the bathroom window are this person's reason for living. It's their way or the highway, and you all roll your eyes when you get a chapter sent into the group chat about a teaspoon being left in the sink. You will fight the urge to drop a Xanax into their cereal.

How to deal:
Make sure you keep common areas (i.e. kitchen, living room, bathroom) clean, but if the demands become too unreasonable, nicely tell them to calm the fuck down.

THE SLOB

If you're looking for a teacup, it's probably gathering mould in their bedroom but good luck finding it in a sea of unwashed clothes. This person is unknowingly breaking the no-pets rule because of the family of four mice that have moved in under their bed. When it's their turn to clean, you learn that people have different definitions of what the word 'clean' means.

How to deal:
It's difficult to teach someone how to be clean. Focus on the common areas and talking to them directly if you want them to change a certain behaviour instead of addressing

the house as a whole. If the mice team up and try to take over the house, side with them because you're more than likely outnumbered.

THE KLEPTO

You could have sworn you just bought that box of cereal. How could it be gone already? No, you're not going insane – there is a sly fox in your midst. Boundary-less creatures who you'll see on a night out wearing a top that you thought you lost two months previously. You start positioning things in certain ways to catch them in the act, but even if you do, they don't admit it. They're probably an actor or a privileged rich person that's tight with money even though Mummy and Daddy pay their rent.

How to deal:

Intervention vibes – they must be stopped. If that doesn't work, draw little sharpie dots on the labels of your clothes, use those Apple AirTag things, and put a note in your cereal that reads, 'I knew you were stealing my cereal – smile for the camera, you kleptomaniac!' You obviously won't have a camera, but you will scare them.

THE PERSON WHO DOESN'T PAY RENT

A romantic partner of one of your housemates who's always in the fucking house but doesn't pay rent. They're almost too comfortable as they throw their legs up on the couch and ask you to make them a cup of tea while you're up. There is more steam coming out of your ears with rage than the kettle. You're fully convinced they don't have a place of their own.

How to deal:

Sit your housemate down and explain to them why it's making you uncomfortable. If that doesn't work, start handing their partner beautifully crafted bills after they stay for extended periods. Offer a mint on departure as well as a link to a Google review page where they can give you feedback about their stay.

Carpet chaos

I went to London to go to dance college so moved there with two dancers from Cork that were on the same course as me. Well, the estate agent saw us coming and we got the mankiest flat I've ever lived in. Our initial clean when we moved in only scratched the surface of what needed to be done. Dirt was so ingrained in the carpet that it nearly resulted in an amputation. Honestly, while I was away one time, one of my housemates and her boyfriend were having sex in the hallway – not sure why it wasn't the bed but to each their own – and he grazed his knee on the carpet. Three days later he was rushed to the A&E because of the pain in his leg. The carpet was so ingrained with dirt and his graze became so infected that he was told they might need to amputate from the thigh down. The infection was life-threatening. (I should mention also that he came from an anti-vax family, so whatever he caught was having a laugh in his body because there were no antibodies in the gaff.) Thankfully, amputation wasn't necessary, but surely this scare would be enough for the landlord to professionally clean the carpet? Well, it wasn't, and we had to do it ourselves. One self-funded professional clean followed by a trip to Dealz and a few coats of Cillit Bang later and the carpet was no longer life-threatening. We could never let the place get like that again, so together with my housemates, we implemented a cleaning rota.

As I type the words 'cleaning rota' I get a shiver down my spine because I never knew a piece of A4 paper stuck to the fridge could cause so much chaos. The idea seemed so simple: each housemate is assigned a common area to clean, and each week it rotates. So, I'll clean the kitchen one week, the living room the next and so on. Should work right? But just like we learned when the public sent Cher Lloyd packing during the 2010 *X Factor* final, people are unpredictable. You see, even with a structured cleaning rota people will have different standards of cleanliness. Similar to how the public had different standards of taste during that *The X Factor* final. At least we got the masterpiece that is 'Swagger Jagger' out of that shambles, though. All I got from my rota was passive-aggressive texts and a sore back from scrubbing the jacks.

As I adapted to living with different types of people my tolerance and understanding grew. People come from all types of upbringings and some of those upbringings don't teach you to replace the toilet paper when it's empty. When Kevin and I moved in together, I realised he was the opposite of the messy housemate. He has a very particular way he wants things done, which I have branded The Kevin Way™ (merchandise coming soon).

THE KEVIN WAY™

Here are just a few of the many rules of The Kevin Way™:

o   Shower curtain must be left on the outside of the bath.

o   Tea towel on the oven must not be used – it's a display tea towel.

o   You must pick up letters in the hall the minute they come in the letter box.

o   Bathroom window must always be open during a shower, even when you have a vent.

o   All mug purchases must be approved by the man himself to avoid cluttering the space.

o   Don't speak during breakfast.

o   Toiletries must be stored in a way that Kevin sees fit.

o   Sit down when you pee. Which, to be fair, was a rule developed out of necessity as I'm admittedly not the best at aiming.

Even though he was tapped, I loved living with Kevin. We just worked as housemates. We were always upfront if the other person was doing something that annoyed us. That's the advice I'd give to anyone who's having issues with a housemate: just be upfront with them. If they keep doing things you said drive you mad then you will have to look into other options, like conducting an elaborate plan to convince them that the house is haunted, but I'd try confronting them head on first.

Hey, Boss Babe

If housemates are one branch you hit when you leave home, employment is another. Well, actually, I've been working since I was 15, when Jordan and I started a grass-cutting business. Two weeks in, I got a job in the local hotel, which offered steady revenue, so ironically I left the entrepreneur life behind and worked as a kitchen porter. I still have nightmares about scraping the scrambled egg off the end of giant pots at 7 a.m. It was tough work, but I was weak that I was earning money, so I took on a load of shifts. I practically lived there. Major life events took place by that sink: I turned 16. I found out a lot of chefs are emotionally unstable and addicted to cocaine. I was even there when the news broke that Michael Jackson had died.

I've always considered myself a work-hard-play-hard kind of gal. Sure, what's the point in earning the money if you're not going to enjoy yourself with it? And, girls, didn't young PJ do just that. As I approached my eighteenth birthday, I moved from the pot wash to the restaurant floor as a waiter. This was my chance to shine. Every table I served was an opportunity to get more tips. Oh, you're American? Well, top of the morning to you, my good sir. It's your birthday? Let me get all the staff together for a song. I was so far in the closet back then I was talking to Aslan, but I would exude camp-waiter energy. The only customers I didn't try to shake down were the old women. We'd a mutual love for one another; they were weak for me and I them. Money had no place in our relationship. Alexa, play 'Love Don't Cost a Thing' by J.Lo because I was just there for the vibes and they were there for the hot-water refills in the pots of tea that I wouldn't charge them for.

Now, I'm making it sound like I was employee of the month, and at the beginning I was. Top tip for anybody starting a job: do everything by the book for the first, like, six months. Then, when you've established the rules and know what role everyone plays, you can get away with murder and they still think you're the workaholic they hired. Once settled into the job at the hotel, I really did take the piss. Most weekends I worked the brekkie shift with a team of equally hungover teens, so we got organised. Two of us would take shifts running the floor while one of us took a nap under the buffet table. We would then rotate who got to sleep every 30 minutes. So, when Room 213 was getting her bowl of Coco Pops, little did she know that under the tablecloth I was getting my forty winks. In my professional opinion, it made us at least 20 per cent more productive and charismatic when we were on the floor, so maybe big companies should adopt this nap/work balance.

I'm convinced that everyone should spend some time working in the service industry. It teaches you respect for the graft that goes into running a restaurant or bar. My friend Sadie and I have worked in the service industry for years and could almost tell you the table numbers of a place and how many covers they turn over a night the minute we step in the door. She knows all the fab new places to eat and drink and I trust all of her recommendations. Why? Because she was a woman on the inside. She gets it, and you best believe that if there is a Karen being mean to a waiter for no reason, we're standing up for the waiter like two lionesses protecting an overworked cub.

LOOKING FOR WERK

In my time I managed to secure an eclectic mix of part-time jobs, which I'll now rate on a scale of one to five. One means it's scarred me for life and five means it was a bit of skit and I've funny stories from it.

Grass-cutting business

Was promising, but Jordan and I couldn't figure out how to work the lawnmower and I jumped ship before it could take off.

Kitchen porter

One of the hardest jobs I've ever had. Picture basically everyone being mean to you as they constantly fill a sink with a never-ending pile of dirty dishes you need to wash while you try to scoop moist food out of the drain.

Waiter

People were still mean but at least I got to perform and play different characters. It's trained me to be the actor/fake bitch that I am today.

Selling wreaths for Christmas

Seasonal work situated outside a shopping centre where hypothermia and frostbite would whisper sweet nothings in my ear as people tried to haggle with me for holly wreaths that I wasn't allowed to sell any cheaper than they were priced. The only saving grace is that I got to work with Dylan and we remixed 'Sleigh Ride' by The Ronettes into a catchy jingle that would rival the work of the top advertising agencies to this day: *'I hear those prices dropping, those wreaths are calling my name* [dum dum dum dum] *Outside is lovely weather for some wreath-buying together with you.'*

Promoter for a strip club

This one was like a fever dream. I was 18 and my job was to get groups of lads from town into the Great Escape strip club. Now, this sounds like it would be any straight teenage boy's dream, but having to approach groups of stags was my nightmare. To top it all off, the rival strip club in Cork, Secrets, used to send out their gorgeous strippers to do their promo. Who do you think the stag is going to go with: the two scantily clad women or the spotty, camp 18-year-old? I was in awe of the strippers. People must have thought I was pure horny for them, but I was just living for their athleticism and girl-boss energy. They would serve puss on the pole, and then work the room to book in their private dances, all while looking stunning. The choreographer in me wanted to give them a few pointers on their routines, but I knew my place. I worked there for a summer and in that time I got to know the regulars. To be honest, the majority of them weren't that creepy, just lonely older men looking for some affection, which, when I thought about it, made me a bit sad.

VIP host

★★★★☆

The first male VIP host in Havana Browns, ladies, gents and my non-binary friends! I was breaking boundaries and working with the hot VIP girls in the club. I would unhook the velvet rope to lead the lucky few into a tiny back bar that didn't feel very important at all. Z-listers would snap their fingers at me to come take their order while they acted all high and mighty, which I always found hilarious. You're in a VIP section of a club in Cork, like, would you calm down? This job gets a high rating though because I could skip the queue and get all my friends in for free on my nights off.

Restaurant supervisor

★★★☆☆

When I first got to London and hit the streets in search of a job, I ended up in a barbeque restaurant in Camden, where I worked for my first few years there. The pros were that the people I worked with were lovely and I could eat and drink whatever I wanted. The cons were that I was depressed and because we could drink whatever we wanted I basically became a functioning alcoholic. So plus one point for the barbeque pork croquettes but minus one point for enabling the downward spiral that was my early twenties.

Children's dance teacher

This job nearly had me booking in to get a vasectomy. I used to teach these really posh, bratty kids in Notting Hill. The yummy mummies would drop off children with names like Chamomile and Parchment before going for brunch while I tried to teach them how to dance. They were unhinged and so privileged. At the end of class, I would kill time by asking them all what they were looking forward to in the coming week. One day, between some sleepover talk and news about a birthday party, one girl says, 'I can't wait to use the credit card my daddy gave me,' and produced an Amex. Readers, she was seven years old.

Host in a restaurant

This job had me drunk with power, girlies. Oh, you want to be rude to me? Sorry, we've no tables. If I like you, window seat. It was almost too much power for me to handle but I was up for the challenge. I could also wear my own clothes in this job, so I was *sliving*.

Advertising creative

Once I got into an advertising agency, I was hooked. The briefings, pitches, campaign launches, client management

– it's all so camp! I loved presenting my work and cosplaying as a queer Donald Draper.

XOXO

Obviously throughout all of this I was still training and working as a professional dancer, but if you think commercial dancers can survive off that work year round, you've watched too many *Step Up* films. I thought I'd be able to live the dream life of the dancers I saw on the big screen, but early in my new life in London I began to realise that those dancers probably had wealthy parents. It's weird because in Cork I was aware that some people were better off than others but it was only when I went to the dance academy that I really saw the difference between myself and some of the other students. For example, I realised some people in their twenties were fully supported by their parents. They hadn't had a part-time job in their lives, which was so bizarre to me. I would go to dance college on Monday straight from a twelve-hour waiting shift the day before, and then one of the unemployed girls at the academy would dare to say she's exhausted and stressed because her ASOS package didn't arrive over the weekend. Now I kind of live for the out-of-touch privileged girlies because it makes me feel like I'm in an episode of Gossip Girl, but when I was exhausted from work and she was banging on about being stressed, I wanted to scream: Shout so loud that the singing teacher at the musical theatre college would come in and give out to me for damaging my vocal cords. I obviously didn't, but can you imagine her face if I did? I didn't know it at the time, but I was discovering what different types of privilege looked like, something I've benefited a lot from as a white cis man. Since then, I've been learning a lot about how people start at different points in the race depending on various factors, and when you weigh it all up, the fact I'd have to work a few extra jobs is nothing compared to what some people have to overcome.

Kevin

Mammying myself

Contrary to what the majority of queer people and allies of the LGBTQ+ community believe about sexuality, I don't think I was born this way. Sorry not sorry, Lady Gaga. A gay thought never crossed my mind until I turned 13 and my uncle Barry and his husband Philip took me to London to see *Wicked*. As the first act came to a close and 'Defying Gravity' reached its climax and Elphaba soared towards the peak of the proscenium arch, something changed within me. *Something was not the same.* I left the Apollo Theatre that day as a homosexual, with a programme to be signed at the stage door in one hand, unable to carry anything in the other now that I was sporting a limp wrist.

I'd spent less than twenty-four hours in London but somehow this unfamiliar city now felt like home. Something in the back of my psyche was telling me that I belonged and it seemed like everything was happening in London and I didn't want to miss out. So when the time finally came for me to move there in 2014, I should have been elated, right? Wrong! I was traumatised. Love that for me! I was a home bird at heart and, in truth, I didn't want to leave my mammy. And Irish mammies don't want their children leaving them either, so in an effort to discourage us from ever flying the nest, Irish mammies have a cunning tactic, whereby they do everything for us for our entire lives so that we don't possess the basic life skills necessary to survive on our own.

Before moving to England, I had never cooked a dinner, used a washing machine, ironed clothes, been grocery shopping by my lonesome or showered myself without the help of my mam. Okay, so I had showered by myself but ultimately I was using the shampoo and conditioner that she had bought and drying myself using the fluffy towels that were freshly laundered and folded in the hot press by her. I had been rendered useless by all of my mam's mammying. Well played, Mam.

My mam accompanied me to London on the day I was making the big move over, and I had a sinking feeling in my stomach from the moment I woke that morning. Pádraig called to the house before I left for the airport to say a last goodbye and when I answered the door I could tell that he had already been crying, as if we were lovers and he was gearing himself up to wave me off to war. I was going off to train to be in a kick line, not the front line, baby. Silly Pádraig. He handed me a letter that was four pages long and a silver chain that had both of our names on it. If he really was my best friend, he would have known that I only wore gold, but I suppose the thought was there.

My mam also wrote me a letter and attempted to hand it to me that evening when she was saying goodbye at the coach station just before she headed back to Cork. I just knew that it was going to break me, and I was already having doubts about being in London and questioning if it was too late to back out. My mam sensed this and upon reading my face when she produced the envelope, immediately put it back into her handbag and said she didn't want me to have it. To avoid any histrionic displays at the bus stop we agreed that she would give it to me a few weeks later when I was more settled and emotions weren't as volatile. She wore sunglasses for the entire journey to the airport to hide her tears, and even thinking about that makes me want to sob.

I loved my new life in London. Homesickness reared its head from time to time, but for the most part I was too busy or too exhausted to be feeling sorry for myself. And I had my own helping of home in the form of a lovely boy from Ennis, called Emmet, so I never felt alone. Myself and

Emmet were the only two Irish people in the year so we were also inevitably the funniest, and laughing got us through many of our difficult days. In first year we struggled to find accommodation and had to settle for living with a landlady who was a bit manic. Her son was also in the house and though he was handsome he was also a brazen pup and definitely could have done with a good smack of a wooden spoon. One time, he had a load of his friends over when his mam was away and I spent the night clutching my pearls as I watched the debauchery unfold. The place was like Lapland with all the coke flying about. Emmet and I were traumatised and tried to turn a blind eye as we tucked into our takeaways and tuned in to *Strictly*.

You better work, bitch

Though our living situation was less than ideal, we weren't too fussed as we didn't spend a great deal of time in the house. We were at college dancing most of the day, and when we weren't dancing we were both working. I wasn't a stranger to hard work and loved the independence that came from earning my own money. I chose violence and got a job in McDonald's because it was nearby and the shift patterns worked with my college timetable and, as one might imagine, it was absolutely chaotic. I was allergic to most of the young lads working in the kitchen and resented the manager for not allowing me to work on the drive-thru, denying me the opportunity to wear the Bluetooth headset and pretend that I was Lizzie McGuire pretending to be Isabella Parigi performing 'What Dreams Are Made Of' live at the Colosseum. The cheek! The day my colleagues found out I was gay they were all shooketh, and the remainder of my shift was spent listening to names of male staff members being called out, with me having to state whether I thought they were hot or not. I would have handed in my notice there and then, but I needed the money and, in truth, the mozzarella dippers had me in an absolute chokehold.

From the summer I turned 16 I made sure I had a part-time job in order to make my own money and to feel a bit independent, putting a percentage of it away on every payday in anticipation of being brought to court for my excessive LimeWire usage. If you're too young to know what LimeWire is, then don't talk to me, please. I worked in a manky café in a shopping centre that also did outdoor catering events, and one time they made me prepare a pig on a spit for a summer fête. I haven't been able to watch *Charlotte's Web* since.

I also worked in a car wash but it wasn't at all fun like the Christina Aguilera and Missy Elliot song from *Shark Tale* suggests. I have tiny hands (but big feet, boys! *wink*), so I was responsible for doing the alloys of the cars and, honestly, it's a wonder I'm even typing this on my laptop right now because my fingers were decimated from it. All the lads would lose the plot when an unreal car came in, and I hadn't a notion about cars (still don't!) and could only ever react to the colour. I remember being at a party when I was younger and waiting around afterwards for my mam to collect me and another boy from my class. He was a bit of a nuisance, but my mam had offered to drop him home as he lived in a nearby estate. While we were waiting, he asked me what type of car my mam drove, and I was like, 'Eh, navy?' He asked what make it was. Sure, I hadn't a notion. He couldn't wrap his head round this and made out like I was thick for not knowing. He then asked me what my dream car would be, and I said I wanted a car that was 'automatic, systematic, *hyyydromatic*' but he didn't get the reference, which only cemented the fact that I knew we could never be friends. 'I don't care, Seán, as long as it's pretty!' I wanted to say. How did this boy who just last week was blessing himself with the wrong hand when we were practising for our first confession know so much about motorised vehicles? His dad must have been a mechanic or a dodgy dealer of wheels like Danny DeVito in *Matilda* without the New York Italian mobster accent. Either way, I was mortified.

Penny-pincher

As I was the one who had made the decision to drop out of university to give the dance thing a go, I became really stubborn and didn't want to accept any handouts from my parents. I come from a working-class background and hated the idea of my mam and dad having to spend their hard-earned cash funding my dreams. I wanted to be the one to make the dream happen for myself. Whenever my parents asked if I was okay for money, I would always just tell them I was grand. This sometimes led to precarious scenarios that I'm sharing here because it feels like a safe space, so don't judge me.

o   I once worked in a Baskin Robbins on Southend seafront, which was next to a Subway. I made friends with the fella who worked there, and at the end of the evening I would give him a few scoops of ice cream in exchange for the leftover meatballs, which I would have with pasta once I returned home.

o   I didn't want to spend money on public transport, so in lieu of getting the bus I travelled around on a fold-up scooter definitely intended for use by an infant, which I had found under the stairs of one of the gaffs I lived at.

o   If I ever had to get the train somewhere I would pay for a child's fare and if I got nabbed by a ticket inspector, I would inflate the Irish accent and tell them I was only over to visit my nan and that we didn't have trains in Ireland, and I usually got away with it.

o   I couldn't be spending money on silly coffees every day, but I was a busy girl and needed my caffeine fix so I signed up to the Waitrose loyalty programme, which meant I was entitled to a free coffee every time I bought something there, which was typically a piece of fruit or a packet of gum.

o Around this time, I was constantly being served ads on my Instagram to become a sperm donor. I'm not going to reveal whether I caved and had a wank out of economic necessity or not, but if you gave birth to a buck-toothed baby with long eyelashes and a touch of rosacea circa 2017, then I hope you're both doing well.

Fake it till you make it

When I graduated, I started working in a pretentious restaurant on Bond Street. The best word I can think of to describe the place and its patrons is 'notions'. Like, the *height* of notions. The menu had things on it like beetroot-cured salmon on blinis and beef onglet, and everyone who set foot in the door sounded like they could have appeared in an episode of *Made in Chelsea*. On my first shift I was asked to debone a man's sea bass, which sounds like a euphemism but I don't think it is. I didn't want to appear incompetent in front of the entire table and decided to give it a go. Sure, it was only a few bones and I had just completed a three-year performing arts degree, so I just pretended like I was acting in one of my improv classes. Did I make shit of the man's fish? Absolutely. Did he suspect I was clueless? Not a chance. Fake it until you make it, girlies! And if a man chokes on a few small bones at lunchtime in Mayfair, it's not the end of the world.

I don't know why, but for some reason gay men make for superb service-industry workers, so it wasn't long before I was running the place. Once I put that apron around my waist, everyone knew I was that bitch. Send your kid to dance classes because, honestly, people think I go above and beyond and do more work than everyone else, when really I'm doing the same work but just have stunning posture, and people can't refrain from putting their trust in you when your spine is as aligned as mine.

Living in London is an expensive gig, and in my first few years of being here I didn't feel like I was *living* in London. I was just existing. I didn't really have much disposable income to do any of the fun things that come with being in a capital city. But I never wanted out. The people I met along the way kept me here and I always felt like I was part of something bigger there. Perhaps I was too stubborn to back out too. Shout-out to all my headstrong Taurus girlies. I'm always getting messages from people who are living in Ireland and are contemplating moving away and looking for advice. A lot of people think about emigrating because of the lure of foreign opportunities and the Oz girlies always look like they're having a scream on their Instagram stories, don't they? Fair fecks to them for making it through the farm work. Could never be me. But people also want to bounce because the Irish government has failed them and they're being priced out of their own country. And leaving home is a big undertaking, right?

In hindsight, I don't know how I had the courage to do so at the age of 21. If you are moving away, don't make too much of a fuss about it and have a big going-away party and tell everyone in the parish of your planned departure. Sure, you might miss out on a few bob from the aunts and uncles but if things go tits-up and you want to come home, you won't be stepping off the Ryanair flight with your tail between your legs. It's not easy, but you have to put yourself out there. If you're Irish, you're already at an advantage, as people automatically assume you're nice when they hear the accent and want to be your friend. Irish people are all over the gaff and we're easy to spot with our big Irish heads and we love to flock together because we can take the piss out of each other without the fear of offence and can talk about the weather to our hearts' content.

A good starting point for striking up a conversation with a fellow Irish person abroad is, 'Do you listen to the podcast *I'm Grand Mam*?' If the answer is no (unlikely), you can assume they are shite craic and you'll want to make a swift exit, but if they do listen, then congratulations, because you've just met your new bestie. Join a group to meet other like-minded people. You could join a sports team or a book club or, if you're in London, come to my Pure Ride spin class where the vibes are always immaculate and the bops are 10/10 and, best of all, you'll get to meet me in the flesh. But no pictures, please, x.

Though it hasn't always been easy, moving away was the best thing I've ever done. And I've never died a winter yet. For queer people especially, there's an even greater desire to emigrate as being the only gay in the village can feel a bit suffocating and opening up Grindr to a grid of headless torsos where you're guaranteed to be related to at least one of them is not ideal. Moving away gives you a fresh perspective, and engaging with new people from different walks of life is so rewarding. Your home will always be there, and any time you return, your mam will make all your favourite dinners. My only request is that if you move to the UK, don't lose your Irish accent and start talking like a Br*t, because that is the height of cringe and you will be disowned. You've been warned.

ARE YOU A KEVIN OR A PJ?

Ever wondered if your personality is parallel with PJ's or closer to Kevin's? Well, now you no longer have to think about it because we've put together a list of very serious questions to help you find out.

1. **When you shower do you open the window:**
a. Beforehand
b. Afterwards

2. **When contemplating whether to make a big purchase do you think to yourself:**
a. 'Hmmm, do I really need this?'
b. 'Feck it, I can't take the money with me!'

3. **If you could date one Disney cartoon prince who would it be?**
a. Aladdin
b. Hercules

4. **If you had to lip-sync for your life to one of the following songs which would you pick?**
a. 'That Don't Impress Me Much' by Shania Twain
b. 'No Scrubs' by TLC

5. **When going on a trip away with friends are you more likely to be the one who:**
a. Plans the whole trip itinerary and keeps the group on track
b. Gets on the flight without even thinking about whether you need an adaptor

6. **Which bottle of wine would you gravitate towards?**

a. Red

b. Rosé

7. **When setting an alarm for the morning do you:**

a. Set just one, knowing that you'll wake the second it goes off

b. Set several in the hopes that one wakes you up

8. **What is your preferred choice of comfy casual footwear?**

a. I'm a Birkenstock bitch

b. Crocs rock

9. **What are your thoughts on sharing a bed with someone?**

a. I couldn't think of anything worse. If I get married I'll have to have my own room away from my partner

b. I've a better night's sleep when I'm wrapped in the arms of the one I love

10. **The waiter has given you the wrong dish at the restaurant. Do you:**

a. Say nothing and eat up

b. Send it back

11. You've an exam coming up. Do you:

a. Create a study plan that you stick to in the lead-up to the exam

b. Cram it all in the night before

12. Growing up, were you more of a:

a. Groovy Chick Girl

b. Bratz Babe

Mostly 'A's? Congratulations! You're a Kevin.

An organised queen who loves systems and schedules. Make sure you marry rich, because having your own bedroom is an absolute need not a want. Every group needs a member who they can rely on to get things done and that girlie is you and you wouldn't have it any other way. After a long day of girl-bossing and sticking to your routine you love to unwind by reading a chapter or two of your book before bed and planning your agenda for the next day!

Mostly 'B's? Step forward the PJs!

You know life's too short, so you say yes to spontaneous trips, impulsively buy the cute top, tell your misogynistic boss to fuck off. There are no filters here, my love, so what you see is what you get. You lead with your heart and romanticise your life to the point where you've gaslit yourself into thinking you're the main character in an award-winning series. 'Work hard play hard' is your motto, babe, so make sure you pack a toothbrush in your work bag because you never know where the day will take you.

SIX

Following your Dreams

'He's away with the fairies.'

NUALA KIRBY

PJ

The bright lights of Sunday's Well BNS

From when I was very young, my mam said I was away with the fairies. A dreamer, if you will. I had an overactive imagination, but what child doesn't? I think the only difference between myself and other kids my age was that my parents never made me feel silly for the stuff I came up with – they just left me off, another by-product of being the youngest child. When I was in my *One Hundred and One Dalmatians* era I was allowed to paint my bedroom white and cover it in black spots, creating a stunning mural that would give Yayoi Kusama a run for her money. Over time, the black dots became teleportation devices and we made a rule that every time you placed your palm on one, it transported you to a different world. My friends and I would play in my room for hours, hitting different spots on the wall that would teleport us to worlds that we made up in our head. I'd say my mam and dad were weak because there was no minding in us – we were happy out.

Growing up in the northside of Cork city, we had youth outreach programmes coming at us left, right and centre to keep us out of trouble and off the streets. One of these programmes was a weekly art class, where we learned how to paint an elephant. I remember my art teacher praising me so much for this painting that at the time I was fully convinced it should have been hung in the Louvre. I found it recently, and I'm lucky someone didn't throw it out thinking it was a dirty piece of paper. Girlies, it was shocking, but it just goes to show how important it is to nurture someone's creativity from an early age. Nobody starts out amazing at something unless you're one of those child prodigies and even they end up unravelling and breaking down unless they have support.

These outreach programs let me explore all different types of creative pursuits. I played Mr Bumble in a local youth club production of *Oliver Twist*. We made stop-motion animations about dealing with depression out of paper and we painted currachs in Meitheal Mara that we took out on the River Lee in summer. Martin Ryan was the legend that ran the youth club, and he really did keep me out of trouble. I enjoyed anything creative, but I was obsessed with performing. Trying to not seem too eager, as I thought it would raise alarm bells, I would put myself forward for things but act like I didn't care if I got them or not.

That was until my primary school teacher, Miss O'Herlihy, announced that we would be putting on a production of *The Lion King*. In that moment, this all-boys' Catholic school might as well have been Broadway. I don't know how she did it, but she managed to convince all of the lads that it was cool to sing, act and dance on stage, which was great news for this closeted little gay boy. Lights, camera, action – it was go time, girls. Jordan and I auditioned together, and when the cast list went up my heart sank when he was cast as Zazu and I got Lion Number Four. I think this was one of the first times I was truly jealous of someone. Putting my jealousy to the side, I decided I was going to be the best Lion Number Four they'd ever seen and tried so hard in rehearsals that Miss O'Herlihy threw me a pity role as Nala's mam a week before the show. The character had one line, but that was one line more than I had before, so I took it with both hands.

'What do you think, Sarabi?' I was supposed to say in response to my cub asking me if she could go to the watering hole. But after opening night, five words weren't enough. If these were my five minutes of fame, I was going to milk them. Second night, I sprinkled three more words on top: 'I don't know, what do you think, Sarabi?' Miss O'Herlihy didn't notice the rewrite, so by the last night I was feeling confident and really got into the character of Nala's mam. What her life was like as a lioness raising cubs in the savannah. What happened in her past that made her have this northside Corkonian accent. I felt like I understood her, and with that came my best line delivery of the whole run. When my daughter asked me to go to the watering hole I replied, 'Well …' pause to build anticipation '… I don't really know …' *slow sigh* '… What do you think, Sarabi?' In my head, the crowd went wild, stood up and gave me a standing ovation as some people wept and threw roses on stage. In reality, the show just continued and Miss O'Herlihy probably regretted giving the overly enthusiastic thespian a line in the first place.

Oh, Honey

This show was the start of a recurring theme throughout my career as a performer. I was never the most talented person in the room – the star blessed with that natural ability to go all the way – but what I was was never afraid to try. I don't know if it is because I always craved other people's approval growing up but if there's one thing I'm going to do, it's work hard for something I want. Jose says it's the Capricorn in me. I'm not really a crystals-and-horoscope girlie, but apparently it tracks. A prime example of this is my dance career.

I didn't start dancing until I was 16. Somewhere between primary and secondary school, people thought it was weird for a fella my age to be away with the fairies doing all sorts of creative projects, so I stopped to protect myself. Everyone loved when lads played sports, so that's what I did. After trying soccer, Gaelic football and hurling, all of which I was equally terrible at, I settled on rugby. I wished someone at the time was like, *Just pick anything else!*

You see, rugby is weird because it's so homophobic while also being the gayest thing I've ever seen. Big beefy lads all wrestling in the mud, lifting each other in the air by the bum, and the biggest ones even do a big group hug that they call a scrum. Like, it's so gay but also you wouldn't dare be a gay man on the pitch. We'd be on the bus going to an away game or, as I liked to call it, standing on a different pitch's side-line for an hour (never got my game, girls) and the lads would be feral. One minute they'd be slapping their dick on someone who'd fallen asleep's face and then calling the fella who was asleep gay because a man's dick was on his face. Meanwhile, the man that was flinging his willy around was a mad thing for whipping it out. It made no sense and was hell, lads, but I played it for four years because my dad was so proud of me and we were bonding, which was so cute. He would be mad chatting to my mam when we got home saying stuff like, 'They were brilliant today, Nuls. PJ got a run and all.' The only reason I got a run was because we were hammering the other team and I couldn't possibly feck things up if I went on.

My sports career got a bit more complicated one rainy day when my mam brought me to the pictures to see the best film of all time, *Honey*. If you don't know what *Honey* is, it's a classic dance film that follows Jessica Alba as she struggles to follow her dreams of becoming a professional dancer. Robbed for the Oscar, if you asked me. Obviously, I'm joking – it's just another one of those cheesy dance films we were bombarded with in the early noughties, but you must watch it if you haven't seen it. Anyway, I left that cinema with a newfound purpose. I was now Jessica, she was now me, and I was going to be a professional dancer. This is when I started my secret training sessions. I used to go to my room and have secret dance classes, learning routines from YouTube videos. I was actually getting better, but nobody could find out.

One time early on in my secret dance career I nearly got caught because I was dancing in my room and thought nobody was home. I was popping, locking, jamming, breaking, unaware that my dad was after coming back. He must have heard the commotion in my room and went to check. When I heard him walking up the stairs, I knew I was nabbed. Panicked, I jumped into my bed but then I realised my dad was just after coming into my room after hearing banging to find me sweaty and flustered under a duvet. It dawned on me that it just looked like I was having a wank. I wasn't going to tell him I was dancing because that was worse. So, I just said I was sick, which we both knew was a lie, and we never spoke about it again.

Big stubborn Capricorn energy

A few years went by, and I finally came out. Not as gay – it took years to unpack that shame. I came out as a dancer because I had found a loophole. I told everyone I was a hip-hop dancer, because that's not gay, that's cool. A white hip-hop dancer from the mean streets of Cork city – very cool. By the time I was filling out the CAO in Sixth Year, I knew I wanted to go to dance college, something that was unheard of in my secondary school at the time. I still remember the guidance counsellor trying to recommend that I study arts in UCC, so I put it down but wasn't convinced. My friend Emma – who is also a dancer – and I both ended up getting into dance college and deferring arts, and we always joked about crawling back to UCC to ask for our place back any time the dance industry wasn't living up to what we thought it would be like. Although I had 'safer' options, all I could think about was dancing. My icon of a French teacher, Miss Harrington, did support the fantasy as long as I learned the language in the meantime, which I thought was a fair trade as for all I knew I could end up dancing in Paris and it would come in handy. There was no protest from my parents, which I know is rare. Traditionally, creative careers in Ireland aren't taken seriously – the arts can be a hobby but you better get a stable 9 to 5 and 'grow up' as soon as you turn 18, so I was lucky that they were okay with the path I took. Not that anyone could have really stopped me, to be fair. I was giving big stubborn

Capricorn energy even back then.

After an eventful Leaving Cert night, where one of the lads got his stomach pumped and Neil Prendeville had every moan in Cork on Red FM that week to talk about it, I closed the secondary-school chapter of my life and it was off to become Jessica Alba. I started my training in the dance course at Coláiste Stiofáin Naofa and, just like in the production of *The Lion King*, I had some work to do. Most of the people in the course had been doing jazz, contemporary and ballet since they could walk. The only other time I heard the term 'turn out' before then was when someone was describing how many people attended a party. I'd come into college early and leave late working on my turns, stretching, choreographing, doing anything to get better. I always felt like I would work harder and had a fiery determination in my belly to get to where I wanted to go.

5,6,7, late?

I quickly learned that to make it as a dancer, you have to leave Ireland. The same parents that were saying the arts are a hobby must also work for the government, because the country just wasn't set up to support artists. So, I auditioned for my dream dance academy in London and cried when I got in. Step aside girls, Nala's mam was off to the big smoke.

London is fucking expensive and while all my former fellow students were getting SUSI grants to go to university,

I was holding fundraisers in the hotel that I used to work in to raise money for the big move. There were deposits to be paid, uniforms to buy and Oyster cards to top up. The local paper even wrote a lead article about me with the headline 'Local Boy from the Northside off to Dance in London'. I said my goodbyes, and after receiving what can only be described as a LIVE LAUGH LOVE-style framed photo collage from Kevin, I was off to London.

This was it. The beginning of the rest of my life. Going from being a big fish in a small pond to a drop in the ocean was such a humbling experience. If I thought I was behind in dance college in Ireland, I didn't even start the race in the UK. These kids were a different breed. While I was learning stupid fucking French at 16, these kids were stretching their oversplits in BRIT schools, which are basically like secondary schools where you spend half the day learning 'normal' subjects and the other half singing, dancing and acting.

I tried not to let it get me down and trained as hard as I could. Unfortunately, this was when the whole passing of my dad was rudely thrown into the mix and the path I had set in front of me for the next three years disappeared. I dropped out of the academy. I couldn't really afford it anyway, and since the funeral everything had just felt different.

The dream wasn't dead – just on life support while I recalibrated. I continued to work in the restaurant in Camden but also got a job in a dance studio, where I'd work on reception and clean the studios in return for free classes. Which I know sounds like the plot of a bad Netflix film, but it's what I did. For years, I'd train in the studio, work in the restaurant and go to auditions. Lads, an anthropologist or someone needs to study the whole auditioning process, because it's insane. I'd be called too tall, not tall enough, too fat but not built enough and concerningly pale all before midday on a random Wednesday – and that's before I've even danced an eight count. I was getting cut from everything I auditioned for, and I could feel my family growing concerned and regretting letting me stay away with the fairies for so long.

My big break

Then it happened: I booked my first big job dancing for this huge pop star. I was giddy and I rang home to tell everyone I was going to be in a music video. It was then I realised I got paid more for doing two shifts in the restaurant than I would get for this video, and my heart dropped. Now, I obviously still did it because I would rather earn money dancing in a music video than fighting with Karen over her undercooked burger, but I knew something needed to change.

I continued dancing for artists, teaching and doing auditions. My career was gaining momentum, but it all felt anticlimactic. I thought that when I became a working professional dancer my life would be fab, but that just wasn't the case. I also felt unfulfilled as I had no creative input in these projects. So, I started exploring other parts of my creativity. I started writing, acting, designing, directing; anything where I could get the creative juices flowing. I started working in creative advertising, which was basically the same as performing arts, if you think about it. I'd act out presentations as if I were on stage, using the skills I've learned from dancing, and they ate it up. It was so fun, and I realised I'd loads of what the business girlies call transferable skills, so I started transferring, babes.

Going from a dance job to a writing job to an art-directing one, I became one of those wanky millennial creatives with a million forward slashes in their job title and confused my poor mam in the process. She still doesn't know what I'm up to half the time. Then myself and Kev started *I'm Grand Mam*, a project we had full creative control over, and that inevitably changed our lives. It was so liberating to take back the power from the audition panels and work on something with my best friend who I knew was a star. Obviously, Kev's my best friend, but he's also an incredible creative partner. Clever, witty, insightful … I could go on for days but I'll save some for our Oscar speech. How he sees the world is completely different to me, but what's weird is that we agree on so much. I feel there is a great balance and that's why we work so well together.

Shoot forward four years, and here I am still doing a million different things, still confusing my mam. I also had a full-circle moment and found my passion for dance again. I'm currently obsessed with teaching my appropriately named 'Throwing Shapes' dance classes in Dublin. Now, I'd be absolutely fucked if there was an apocalypse because I've no practical skills. Nurses, builders and farmers, you will save us when the world finally has enough of our carry-on and decides to check out. I don't think my interpretive dance will do much good, but I am learning how to make kombucha, and even if the world is exploding, people will still need to manage their IBS, you know? So, there's that. Jesus, I'm a walking stereotype, aren't I?

It's always after a few glasses of wine that people's lips start to loosen and you hear about their dreams. This is usually the point at which I turn into their biggest cheerleader, minus the glam outfit and stunning pompoms. I want to encourage my friends like people did for me when I was young. You'll have enough naysayers in your life – try to find the fairies.

Kevin

A star is born

In Senior Infants, when the other kids were preoccupied with picking their nose and busy biting the ends off the sleeves of their school jumper (which used to SEND me), I took it upon myself to write a book. I don't want to use the term child prodigy, but I also don't want to *not* use it. The book was all about what I wanted to be when I was older and the teacher knew I put my whole HB pencil into writing it, so she had it bound for me and everything, so I legitimately felt like I was in my author era. In it, I basically listed out different professions that I was drawn to and said what I liked about each of them and what made me suited to each role. There was no mention of a policeman or a fireman or a footballer, which probably would have been popular choices of my peers, but those careers didn't appeal to me. If you were to read my book, two things would have been abundantly clear: that my handwriting was actually kind of stunning and definitely advanced for a child of my age and, secondly, that I wanted to be a star. I was absolutely away with the fairies.

When we were in Fifth Class, our teacher decided to put on a production of *Oliver!* and somehow I was overlooked for one of the main roles. I'm definitely not still bitter about it, but I'd just like to say that the boys who were picked to be main characters weren't at all talented and didn't know their downstage from their upstage. When the boy playing Oliver was singing 'Where is Love?', all that was going through my head was 'Where is the note, girl?', because it all sounded very pitchy. There must have been backhanders happening behind the scenes from the parents and one of the lads' mams was also a teacher in the school, so that must've been why he was picked. Nepo-baby energy.

I was sullen and sour but found solace in the sentiment that there are no small parts, only small actors, and though I just had the one line as one of the unnamed funeral directors, I was determined to shine on that stage and make Ms Walsh regret not putting my name on that casting notice next to the part of the Artful Dodger. *Consider yourself* full of remorse, Ms Walsh. My line was, 'We were looking for a boy, actually. He could help out with the funerals and all,' and I delivered it with gusto and gumption.

The following year, Cork Opera House announced that they were having an open call for a professional production of *Oliver!* that was happening in the theatre that summer, and myself and Pádraig were buzzing. It was my shot at redemption, and I already knew all the lyrics to all the songs for the audition. I smashed the first round, and as a 'well done' my mam took me to get a pack of those sugary donuts that they used to make fresh in front of you in that bakery on Paul Street. I was a bit chubby at the time, and because I was auditioning for one of the workhouse children who subsisted on a diet of gruel, I decided not to finish all of the donuts. It's giving method.

The next week, we had the recall, where we had to do some more singing and more movement as taught to us by Bryan Flynn, who was directing the production. Some of the most talented children in the city were there, but I felt like I was holding my own and was spurred on further by the desire for vindication. We were at the last hurdle, and a group of about sixty of us were asked to come in again later that evening. Another trip for some sugary donuts to keep the energy levels sustained. When we went back in, we were called up to the stage of the Opera House, and I remember being completely overwhelmed by the scale of it.

We were split into two groups and were all convinced that one group represented the cast and the others would be sent home, like an episode of *Pop Idol*. It was all very dramatic. Pádraig was in the other group, and I remember thinking that I would have been absolutely rotted if he got it and I didn't. But it turns out the show was being double-cast and everyone on that stage was booked and blessed. We got the gig, girls! The show was the best experience and honestly such a formative point in my life. I still get chills when I listen to the *Oliver!* soundtrack.

What's for you won't go by you

I know it's not the quote for this chapter, but my mam has always said, 'What's for you won't go by you,' and I believe in that wholeheartedly. There's comfort in it when you're faced with setbacks and feel like your dreams aren't playing out the way they're supposed to. When I was auditioning for dance colleges in London, I had my heart set on one school in particular. Their pupils had a reputation for being prim, proper, professional and impossibly pretty, and their alumni could be seen gracing the pages of every programme for every show in the West End. I knew I did a good job in my first audition with the hinting smiles from the panel, who all seemed to be willing me to do well.

I was already imagining myself as a student there and had made a mental note of where I would take a picture on my very first day in my new pair of Bloch split-sole jazz sneakers, to let people know that I was now part of the elite. The school got in touch that same week to tell me that I had been accepted, and though I was in hysterics, I wasn't able to celebrate just yet. I was invited back for a second-round scholarship audition, which would determine whether I would receive funding to attend the school or not. And girlies, I needed that money. The fees at the time were around £8,500 a year, so unless I got a smack off a car or had a slip inside SuperValu, there was no way I could have come up with the funds.

For the scholarship audition I had to prepare a solo dance routine to music of my choosing. I picked an instrumental version of Macklemore's 'Same Love'. When I was in the closet, I used to listen to the song and mouth the lyrics while looking in the mirror and having a bit of a cry for myself. That sounds sad, but I'm honestly screaming thinking about it. I performed my routine for the founder of the college and other members of the dance faculty. There was also a third-year boy in the room who was operating the music, and I danced better than I ever did because he was watching and he was only handsome. I was breathing quite heavily but trying to disguise it because I didn't want them thinking I was unfit.

The founder raised her head and asked me if I'd choreographed the routine myself. I said I did and there seemed to be nods of approval between the panel. She then asked if the dance was about the IRA, and my stomach nearly slipped out of my ass. What the heck? How in the name of Christ did she get that from the routine? I told her, absolutely not, and went on a bit of a ramble about how I had struggled with my sexuality and that I had recently come out to friends and family. There was a long, awkward pause in the room. Eventually she came out with, 'Oh, I thought it was about the IRA.' What an eejit.

The following week, my mam messaged me to let me know that my letter had arrived. I was studying in Coláiste Stiofáin Naofa in Cork, and she drove up to the school on the Tramore Road to give it to me. She seemed just as nervous as I was. She was also just as devastated as I was when I opened it up and learned that I hadn't received a scholarship. I was crushed. I was no longer away with the fairies; my wings had been well and truly clipped, and the harsh reality of not attending my dream dance college sent me tumbling back to earth. But if there's one thing I learned from Nadine Coyle lying about her age and losing out on a spot in the band Six only to go on and become part of one of the most successful girl bands of all time, it's that a 'no' isn't necessarily the end of the road. The universe has bigger plans for you.

I still had funding rounds of auditions left for other schools and trusted in my mam's words. And a few weeks later, another letter came in the door, and this time it was good news: I had received a scholarship to attend Masters Performing Arts that September. A whole new chapter awaited me, along with a load of other fairies who were chasing the same dream.

Ship happens

When I was making the decision to drop out of UCC to pursue musical theatre, the line, 'Do something you love and you'll never have to work a day in your life' dominated my thoughts. I would like to have a word with whoever first coined this phrase, as I believe them to be a liar. They lie like a rug! Liabetes! I think that, whatever career path you end up pursuing, regardless of how passionate you are about it, it still feels like work. This became particularly apparent when I undertook my first professional contract working as a production dancer on a cruise ship. It was one of the first auditions I had after graduating, and I was buzzing about the prospect of travelling around Asia for free while getting to save a few bob. And though I had never been on a cruise, I knew they were giving glamour and luxury. However, it wasn't all plain sailing (proud of that one). Though I did have a hull of a time, there were a few things that happened on the cruise (listed below) that I wasn't ferry fond of. But ship happens. That's the last of the puns, I promise.

o   I completely underestimated how difficult it would be dancing on a moving ship. Seasickness is very much a thing, and I was forever falling all over the place. If any footage from the shows was to surface then I would probably have to go into hiding.

o   There are hangovers and then there are cruise hangovers, and if you have never experienced the latter, I envy you.

o   I didn't kiss a boy in six months.

o   I was responsible for maintaining all my costumes for the show and, oh my god, there were so many sequins. My fingers were fecked from sewing.

o   We did a show in the casino on the ship, where people were allowed to smoke and, honestly, it used to make me sick.

o   Because of the language barrier, it was near impossible to get a decent haircut in any of the ports. On one occasion I paid 40,000 yen in Japan in what I thought was a glam hair salon only to realise I had paid for a half-hour-long head massage.

o   We had to pay for internet on the ship, which meant that there wasn't a whole lot of communication with my friends and family back home.

o   A lot of the routines relied heavily on partner work, so I was constantly lifting people over my head or swinging people around the gaff, and my shoulder rotator cuffs were like, 'Really, girl?'

o   On one occasion, I thought I pulled my hamstring mid-show. I heard a harrowing snap when I did a kick and crawled off-stage, sobbing, thinking my dancing career was over before it had even begun. Turns out one of my braces popped off my trousers, but it was still pretty traumatic.

o   We had to be clean-shaven, so I spent the duration of my time on the ship looking like a foetus.

o   One of the shows featured a lot of the songs from the movie *Burlesque* and it completely ruined the soundtrack for me.

o   I had to share a tiny room with one of the other male dancers. He was from Bulgaria and watched *Home Alone* for the first time when on the ship and used to always scream my name the way Catherine O'Hara called for Kevin in the movie when she's on the plane and realises they left Kevin at home. He also clipped his toenails in the room, which used to send me into orbit.

o   There wasn't any decent coffee on the ship but, to be fair, the banana bread was stunning.

o   The majority of the passengers were Chinese and typically elderly, and many of them hadn't seen Westerners in person, so used to incessantly ask me and the rest of the cast for photos. My head was wrecked.

O   We had to do a lot of training on the correct procedure
     to follow if pirates ever invaded the ship. Did you think
     pirates weren't real? Me too! Turns out they're still a thing
     and they're as petrifying as one might imagine and don't
     have cute parrots on their shoulder to take the edge off.

The big break

When I finished on the cruise I returned to London and
started auditioning again and was determined to make the
dream happen. I still had huge ambitions for the way in which
I saw my career as a performer being carved out and I was
spurred on further by declarations from friends on Instagram
who were 'delighted to announce' that they would be joining
the cast of a particular West End show. It was around this time
that PJ and I started doing the podcast, with the ambition of
it being a creative assignment we could both work on together
in our spare time while we were waiting for our big break.

I didn't realise it at the time, but starting *I'm Grand Mam*
was our big break. It's our own passion project, and we're the
performers, the directors and the ones writing the script.
And the best thing about it is I've gotten to do it with my
best friend by my side. And even though it has been a lot of
work, it's been so worthwhile and I'm extremely proud of us
both. One of the things I really admire about PJ is his tenacity.
In the early years of working together I had a tendency to
over-analyse things and think about what would happen if

plans went wrong, whereas PJ's approach was to always jump in head first without any fear of failure. Imposter syndrome would sometimes set in, but PJ never let her stay. We gave Naomi Campbell a run for her money on photoshoots, lived our pop-star fantasies when we recorded and shot the music video for *Fast Lane*, went on tour, performed at festivals, have been on *The Late Late Show* and, look at us now, writing a book.

I never used to like being told I was away with the fairies. But essentially you're just being called out for being a bit of a dreamer, and where's the harm in that? And if you think about it, fairies are kind of stunning, aren't they? And can we take a moment for fairy cakes? Understated and delicious. As we get older, we tend to become a bit more pragmatic about things and are less inclined to take chances because of a fear of failing or making a bit of a fool of ourselves, and we don't dare to dream as much but, sure, that's no fun. Let's follow the fairies and if it all goes tits-up and you end up being caught out on national telly when you give your actual date of birth ('15th of the 6th 1985, making me a Gemini') and have to pretend to not be able to find your passport, who cares? Next time I'm going on holidays, I'm changing my OoO (Out of Office) auto-reply email to AwTF (Away with The Fairies). Nicer ring to it.

PAUL MESCAL FAN FICTION

A dream come true for us was getting Paul Mescal on the podcast. Oscar and Emmy nominee, BAFTA and Olivier Award-winning Paul Mescal. We were talking about how much we loved the series *Normal People* on the podcast and Kevin was completely thirsting over Paul and how much of a ride he is. When the podcast was released, we received an email from his lovely agent Lara, who told us that she and Paul were big fans of the podcast and asked if we would be interested in interviewing him. We'd never had a guest on the podcast and now we had landed a chat with 'the hottest ticket in town'. Though we were in an absolute heap, it was an invitation we couldn't turn down, and it resulted in one of our favourite episodes to date. Here is some homoerotic fan fiction based on the series that somehow made its way into the episode:

THE CAST

Connell: Paul Mescal

Niall: Kevin Twomey

Rude French waiter: PJ Kirby

Connell and Niall have gone inter-railing. As part of their travels, they end up in Paris, where they share a baguette and some cheese, drink a lot of gorgey wine and find them- selves being slowly seduced by the city's allure. In this scene, they are in a restaurant on the banks of the Seine.

Connell: I feel like we've been waiting ages for our food and the waiter just keeps ignoring me.

Niall: He's very rude, isn't he?

Connell: I just don't understand what's taking them so long!

Niall: Let me try and get his attention. Eh, excuse me?

Waiter: Oui?

Niall: I was just wondering if our food is nearly ready. We ordered nearly an hour ago and we're starving.

Waiter: I am not cooking your food, so I have no idea when it will be ready. But as soon as it is ready, I will bring it out, sir.

Niall: Well, in the meantime, can we get another bottle of red for the table, please?

[Waiter leaves abruptly and rudely]

Connell: So rude, like. I really didn't like the way he spoke to you. And his French accent seems a bit suspect.

Niall: Don't worry about it, Connell. Let's just try and enjoy the rest of our evening. We've had such a lovely day and I don't want this to spoil it. What's been your highlight of Paris?

Connell: Hmmm, I loved the Louvre yesterday. I could have looked at some of the paintings in there for the whole day, they were so beautiful.

Niall: I know the feeling.

Connell: What?

Niall: I said they were so appealing.

Connell: Yeah. What about you?

Niall: Probably the Eiffel Tower last night. I just thought it was really romantic with all the lights and everything. I'm glad I got to experience it with you.

Connell: Yeah me too, Kevin – I mean, Niall.

Niall: Though I don't think I'll ever come back to Paris, because the service is so shocking.

Connell: Yeah, this is a joke. What do you say we make a run for it? As soon as the waiter drops over the bottle of wine, we take it and leg it.

Niall: What about the food? I'm starving.

Connell: We'll get something in McDonald's on the way back to the hostel. We'll eat that, drink the bottle of wine, then I just have to douche quickly before we head out.

Niall: [excitedly] Douche?!

Connell: Yeah – it's French for shower.

Niall: Oh ...

Connell: So, what do you say – are you up for it?

Niall: I've never done anything like this before, but when I'm with you I feel ... I feel ...

Connell: Chaotic?

Niall: Yeah ...

SEVEN

Finding Joy

'What's the point
if you're not
enjoying yourself?'

PHIL TWOMEY

Kevin

The best thing that has come from doing the podcast is bringing joy to other people's lives. We regularly get messages from people who have reached out to tell us that they were going through a rough time and that listening to the podcast has helped them feel a bit more positive. Who needs therapy, huh? (That's a joke, by the way, we're both big advocates for therapy if you can afford it.) The big plus of going to therapy is being able to start sentences with, 'Well, my therapist said' followed by something that absolutely did not come out of your therapist's mouth. Another is using, 'My therapist told me you would say that' as a rebuttal when PJ says something I disagree with. When we record the podcast together we honestly have such a laugh, and the fact that our listeners can tap into this too is so satisfying. Growing up listening to people's prejudice towards gay people had us resenting ourselves. The (few) queer stories that we got to see play out on TV were disconcerting ones and had us thinking that we would share the same fate. There's a bit of a bleakness that tends to typify queer cinema, and it can be a bit exhausting. Of course, these stories are important and they illustrate that we're a community of resilience, but we also think it's very important to share the joyous stories so that there's hope for the next generation. And also because being gay can be an absolute scream. And nothing is a bigger scream than a gay night out.

Big Gay Nights Out with the girlies, gays and theys

Going on a night out with your friends is the perfect escape from reality. You get to switch off from the outside world and your only task is to make sure you have a good time and know all the choreography to Whigfield's 'Saturday Night'. It's you and the girlies coming together and connecting through music and dance and shape-throwing-induced sweat patches. This uniting of individuals is particularly important for members of the queer community where clubs act as a safe space; a refuge for us to come together and celebrate our differences in a place where we can be ourselves. We don't need to be on high alert and can let our defences down. Anything goes. I don't have to stress about the fact that I'm wearing a crop top or stop myself from using my hands too much when I speak or worry about diluting my dancing.

When I was in Fourth Year in school, we did a TY musical, which was our own take on *The Wizard of Oz*. For the finale, we did Alexandra Burke's 'Bad Boys', a song I was obsessed with at the time. Because the show was being choreographed by our PE teacher, who didn't have a background in dance, we just copied the choreography from the music video and, of course, I already knew every step. When it came to performing it, I didn't put my whole bussy into it because I didn't want to draw too much attention to myself. Sounds ridiculous, I know, and realistically all eyes were probably on me, as I was positioned front and centre and was wearing Dorothy's signature blue gingham dress, which, to be fair, did look stunning on me. I was annoyed at myself for holding back and letting the fear of judgement from others dull my shine. So, for the last show, you best believe I put those ruby slippers through their paces and gave my everything. Though I was up to ninety, I felt incredible for it afterwards, like I had unlocked my superpower. ('You've always had the power, my dear, you just had to learn it yourself.') But, typically in non-queer spaces, I would revert back to toning things down in order to feel safe. When I'm with my girlies at a queer club, this isn't a cause for concern. Once I came out to friends and family, going to a gay club was my next port of call. In Cork we weren't exactly spoiled for choice, but we did have Chambers down Washington Street, which has been a safe haven for the LGBTQ+ community in the city ever since it opened back in 2006. Previously, if I was ever walking past the venue I would have to stop myself from trying to peer in, so as not to appear overly curious. But the allure of the unknown was too strong. Just like Adam in the Garden of Eden, I was ready to be led astray – only in this story we have a drag queen tempting me with a strawberry daiquiri in lieu of a snake with an apple. But once I set foot inside, I felt like I belonged.

Lads weren't jumping on each other's backs and there wasn't a smell of Joop. People danced in time with the music and were really going for it, without fear of ridicule from others. There were pride flags and pictures of LGBTQ+ trailblazers on the walls. There was laughing and lip-syncs and actually some form of a system when queuing for drinks, and the best thing was that if I spotted a fella I fancied I didn't have to worry about him coming over to slide-tackle me if my eyes lingered a bit too long. And, oh my god, the music. It was as if someone had hacked my Spotify and curated a playlist of all my favourite songs to have a bop to. And have a bop I did.

QUINTESSENTIAL LISTENING FOR
A NIGHT ON THE TILES

o   'Into You' – Ariana Grande
o   'Sound of the Underground' – Girls Aloud
o   'Dancing on My Own' – Robyn

o   'Step by Step – Junior's Arena Anthem Radio' –
    Whitney Houston, Junior Vasquez

o   'Break My Soul' – Beyoncé

o   'Padam Padam' – Kylie Minogue

o   'Buttons' – Pussycat Dolls

o   'Fergalicious' – Fergie

o   'Gimme More' – Britney Spears

o   'It's Raining Men' – The Weather Girls

o   'Rain on Me' – Lady Gaga, Ariana Grande

o   'Touch' – Little Mix

o   'Fast Lane' – I'm Grand Mam

Going out to a gay club could even be described as cere-
monious. There's a ritual of uniting with your friends on
the dance floor, which somehow feels like home. LGBTQ+
people seek sanctuary in these spaces. For some people,
holding the hand of a loved one in public can feel like an act
of defiance and can be quite scary, but inside the walls of a
gay club, this is not a fear. When I moved to London, I was
spoiled for choice when it came to options for a gay night
out and some of my favourite memories from my time in
the city were made on nights out with PJ and our friends
Furquan and Ryan. Dollar Baby at Metropolis was absolute
scenes with the most stunning go-go dancers, and a night
there would typically culminate with a dip in the jacuzzi on
the top floor, which meant having to get the Tube home with

our jocks in our hands. Working Men's Club in Bethnal Green with its iconic pink neon heart on stage always had the nicest crowd and did amazing cabaret shows. I'd always wake up battered and bruised the next morning after a night there, having attempted some kind of routine on the pole, because you best believe my mam didn't raise a wallflower. Hard Cock Life, or HCL for short (and the name I use when discussing the event with my mam), is one of my favourite club nights with the best hip-hop and R'n'B music. And many an evening started off with a naive notion of going for a casual drink in Dalston and ended up being a night of debauchery and chaos with the gays and theys in The Glory or Superstores. Boy, were they worth it.

Queer clubs really do possess the blueprint for a great night out, so it's no surprise that heterosexual people are suffering from FOMO and are looking to get in on the action. For straight girls in particular, these spaces act as a refuge from the prying eyes and unwanted advances of straight males. However, there is a certain etiquette for non-queer people that should be adhered to when occupying these spaces. As a starter, I would just question your reasoning for wanting to attend a queer space when they are already in limited supply. There are more straight bars in the world than I've had hot dinners. Is it simply because you're a fan of RuPaul's *Drag Race* and you want to witness a death-drop in person? Not a great reason, imho. A good place to start would be if you maybe have one queer friend in your peer group and you want to accompany them on a gay night out because you're an ally and want to be there for support and be their wing-woman when they're looking to pull. We stan this type of behaviour.

BEHAVIOUR WE DO NOT STAN

If you're straight in a queer space, bear in mind the following:

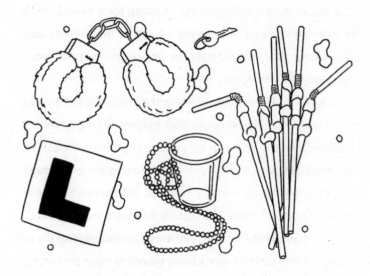

0   Don't arrive in a sash-wearing, cock-straw-sucking, tiara-topped flock. I am, of course, referring to hen parties. A queer space is somewhere we can go to finally be the majority.

o   If you are not part of our tribe and you invade our space, it can make us feel like we're some sort of spectacle under scrutiny. Just because the DJ is playing Britney's 'Circus' doesn't mean that the gay club is one.

o   No unsolicited touching, especially when it comes to drag queens. Self-explanatory. If you do, you run the risk of getting slapped and there's a high chance the footage could end up on TikTok and you'll be cancelled and your HR team will be notified and you'll lose your job. Stressful, right? So, no touching.

o   And when the drag queens are performing, don't take it upon yourself to join them on stage unless you're invited. Just because you go to a weekly Zumba class with your co-worker Aisling and the instructor has stated that you have fab rhythm doesn't mean you've to showcase it, my love.

o   Eliminate the following phrases from your vocabulary before entering a queer space:

   o   'Yassss, Queen' – sends shivers down my spine when I hear it and it's not being used ironically.

   o   'I never would have guessed you were gay'
   – despite what you may think, this is not a compliment.

   o   'If you weren't gay I would definitely get with you' – huh?

o 'I must introduce you to my other gay friend' – just because you have a gay friend does not mean that I want to meet them. Well, unless they are really, really hot.

o 'Tell me your coming-out story' – some people in queer spaces may not be out to friends and family. This is their opportunity to switch off and forget about all that. Similarly, people who are out probably don't want to be reliving this on a night out.

o 'I'm practically a gay man in a woman's body' – No you're not, Gráinne. So you watched *Smash* and love Laura Dern. That doesn't make you a gay man.

o 'I've always wanted a gay best friend, will you be mine?' Absolutely not. I met you five minutes ago, Niamh, and you've already spilled half your vodka Red Bull on my top.

o Don't buy yourself a drink without offering to buy me one too. It's just manners.

o Don't request any songs from the DJ. You have forfeited your right. We don't care if your friend Róisín is going through a break-up and you want 'Single Ladies' to be played in solidarity with your grieving girlie. It isn't happening, Sasha Fierce.

o This last one is for the lads – the hetty lads. If you are being an ally and going to one of these spaces to support a friend, and you're hot, then it's likely that you will be hit on. Let the person down nicely without being insulting, and take it as a compliment. The person managed to see past your choice of footwear and limited two-part skincare routine of Nivea For Men face wash and Bulldog moisturiser and still continued with their pursuit. You must be quite the catch.

Though going on a gay night out is an absolute laugh and a half, it would be nothing without the company of my friends, my chosen family. They're the ones who understand me, support me and celebrate me, and I do the same for them. Life can be shit, but if you surround yourself with the right people at least you can laugh about how shit it can be over a cuppa or a glass of wine.

Camp, culture, community

It's so important to have these spaces to assimilate and celebrate, to see ourselves in each other and connect over our shared struggles and mutual appreciation of Paul Mescal and poppers. It's camp. It's culture. It's community. Of course, there is also a need to have spaces where we can do all of the above in the absence of drink. Too often the social queer experience tends to revolve around alcohol and drugs, resulting in a large subset of the community being ostracised. People who are under the age of 18 and those who don't drink for religious, health or economic reasons are all excluded, as well as people who are battling addiction. Studies have found that lesbian, gay and bisexual people are significantly more likely than straight people to report alcohol and drug misuse. Sober spaces, like queer cafés, LGBTQ+-friendly sporting societies and book clubs, ensure that all members of the community are being catered for.

In London, I joined Stonewall FC and played five-a-side football with them for two years. It all sounds very masc but the team was actually very accepting and I felt really empowered returning to football, having fallen out of love with the sport when I was coming to terms with my sexuality. In my teens, I played with Tramore Athletic FC, a club that my brother, dad and other members of my family were heavily involved with. When I was around 13, I had gotten into the children's chorus in the pantomime *Babes in the Wood* and I was weak for myself (though I was definitely half-seething that I was only a chorus girl and not one of the babes). Once at a training session with Tramore, the coach announced that we had a match that Sunday and wanted to know if anyone couldn't make it. I had a matinée that Sunday (the glamour!) and obviously couldn't miss it. I knew I had to say something. I put my hand up and said I wouldn't be there as I was performing in the pantomime in the Opera House. I thought this would garner respect and possible applause amongst my team mates, but instead had the opposite effect and resulted in my teammates breaking out into hysterical laughter. Philistines! So, returning to a sport that had once made me feel 'other' and being welcomed by like-minded people who had probably at one point been made to feel the same as I had felt ... right. And there were also some boys there who looked really cute in the kits, which also felt right. It was also a great way to make new friends.

You're never too old to make new friends, though the task of having to put ourselves out there can feel daunting. As Irish people, we tend to get a bit mortified for ourselves, and the fear of rejection keeps us from making the effort in the first place. At the start of this year, I joined Crossfit, partly because I wanted to switch up the type of training I was doing, but mostly so that I could mention it on my Tinder and Hinge profiles. I also wanted to learn how to handstand because – and don't come for me – I think it's kind of sexy? It was the first time in years that I was thrust into a new social setting where I didn't know anyone and most people already knew each other, and even though I'm well able to talk to people, I was a bit shook. I was the boy on holidays who didn't really make friends. I couldn't fathom how anyone did. But I think you just have to trust the notion that everyone is happy to make new friends, especially if you're a lovely person. And cities can be lonely places, so typically an opportunity to expand one's social circle is welcomed.

Respecting and connecting with your elders

The more I connect with different members of the LGBTQ+ community, the more apparent it is just how much we all have in common, regardless of how different our backgrounds are. It is these shared struggles and circumstances that help us to understand each other more and empathise with one another. There is also so much that we can learn from older members of the community. No, I'm not talking about PJ, though he does look very old, doesn't he? On a recent trip to Sitges, myself, PJ and Pádraig got talking to three older gentlemen from the States down on the gay nude beach. We didn't know beforehand that clothing was optional but it quickly became apparent that was the case, because we saw more willies than grains of sand that day. I opted to keep my speedos on, for fear of getting the small fella sunburned. Charlie, Karl and Richie were from Palm Springs and struck up conversation with us because we were the only ones bringing the vibes. Charlie had worked as a costume designer on a few Broadway shows, so I was obviously obsessed. He had so many interesting stories to share and, sure, we were only happy to listen as we drank sangria and soaked up the Spanish sun. We told them that if we ever go to America, we'll pay them a visit because we were so fond of them (and also because I'm mad to have a lamp of their gaff, of course).

So much of our queer liberation is down to the people who came before us and engaged in radical direct action to combat discrimination against the community. The very first Pride was actually a riot and happened when patrons of the Stonewall Inn in New York City fought back against a police raid. It launched a new era in gay rights activism. Closer to home, homosexuality was only decriminalised in Ireland in 1993, the year myself and PJ were born (but PJ looks much older, right?), following a lengthy legal battle taken by David Norris against the Irish State to the European Court of Human Rights. Trans activist and trailblazer Dr Lydia Foy also battled the courts for her rights and paved the way for gender recognition legislation in Ireland. More recently, the 'accidental activist' Panti Bliss played an instrumental role in the campaign for marriage equality in Ireland, and I will never tire of watching her Noble Call speech at the Abbey Theatre.

I was in a very fortunate position to have my uncle Barry, an out and proud gay man, as a role model when I was younger. It's hard to be what you cannot see, and I was so lucky because I got to see him loads. He lived with my nan, and when I would go to the house I would get to watch *The Sound of Music* or *The King and I* or some other musical from his VHS collection. I got to attend his and his partner Philip's civil ceremony when I was a teenager. It was such a crucial moment in my journey to self-acceptance: getting to witness a day when all my family came together to celebrate two men who loved each other. And, let's face it, the gays just do parties better, don't they? It showed me that joy is possible at a time when I really needed to see it. At a time when it feels like our community is facing seemingly insurmountable odds, it can be difficult to see past the hate and the hardship and find joy, but we have to. We owe it to ourselves, and we owe it to the other members of our community.

PJ

Celtic Tiger trauma

After reading Kevin's half of this chapter I want to slam this laptop closed, grab some drinkies and hit the tiles with the queers. I've been obsessed with a good party for as long as I can remember. Even as a child, I'd be the last on the bouncy castle, high on soft drinks and birthday cake. To this day, I'm mad for a shindig. I just love being surrounded by my friends and not feeling like I've to rush off to do something. My whole life I struggled with feeling like I'm not working hard enough. Growing up in a time where girl-boss culture and capitalism were glorified, I learned that your worth was based on how well you were doing in your profession. My default, even to this day, is to feel like I need to constantly be working on the next project or I'll lose everything. I should definitely speak to a therapist about this, but I don't have time because I've filled every second of the week with work I need to get done. Maybe the collapse of the Celtic Tiger into the recession traumatised me a bit? Maybe I'm just a greedy little shit? Anyway, I really struggle to relax and do nothing.

I'm trying to address it because being a slave to capitalism is not chic and I give myself the ick. I think that I'm just scared because of how unstable a creative career is. When I first started out as a professional dancer, I was told that it's a difficult road – and they were right. It perpetuated this destination-based mentality that is ingrained in me to this day. When I felt like I was failing, I'd always reiterate my goals to myself. *When I get booked as a dancer in a music video, I'll be happy. When I start earning money from my creativity, I'll be happy.* This way of thinking started to seep into other areas of my life. *When I get a six-pack, I'll be happy. When I move into a nicer place, I'll be happy.* The problem was that when I started to achieve all these goals I was like, *OMG, I've been scammed*, because I still felt the same. This triggered a cycle of me gaslighting myself into sacrificing my well-being to reach a goal for one adrenaline hit before I'd go back to feeling a bit meh and have to quickly find a new one to focus on.

Initially, this is why I loved going out. When you're out clubbing with friends, you don't have time to think about hustling and grinding to reach your goals. Also, when I was hungover, I would be able to give myself permission to slack a bit and relax in a way that I never could if I was feeling 100 per cent. Nowadays when I go out, it's just for fun, but back then I was going out to escape the boss-babe life that I had curated for myself. I think as I came into my late twenties I started to question my way of living and my mindset began to shift. Like a lot of people, I had time to think during the lockdowns, and goal-based happiness is now much less important to me. Don't get me wrong, I still have goals I want to achieve but I'm trying to separate those achievements from my self-worth and happiness. Maybe it's a thing that comes with age, but Phil's saying, 'What's the point if you're not enjoying yourself?' really is something that I now live by.

Life can be so tough, right, and it can change in two seconds. We lose loved ones, are let go from our jobs, have to move out of our homes, and it makes me think, *What's the point in waiting to find joy?* I know I'm oversimplifying things, and people find themselves in so many different circumstances that would prevent them from doing this, but this mindset is what's currently working for me. I'm learning to find joy in wholesome everyday bits, like having a biccie after dinner even though you're full because you obviously still need something sweet. But there are also ways of thinking that I now value way more than I did in past. And the first one is that I'm not that important.

Now, don't get me wrong, I still have self-worth, but I remind myself that I'm not more or less important than anyone else. This has removed the mentality that we're all racing against each other and the only way to get ahead is to hustle and gatekeep. There's enough space at the table for everyone, so if people could just pop a Xanny and realise that just because someone is doing well doesn't mean that you're doing shit, then we can all just have a skit and not put too much pressure on ourselves to overtake the person next to us. Turning the rat race into a stunning camp frolic.

Although it's very easy to feel stuck in the life that you're currently in, it is possible to shake it up. Absolutely terrifying but possible. Take my friend Beverly, for example – two years ago she wasn't liking where her life was heading. After quitting her job, a break-up and a quick Skyscanner search, she was off travelling the world for the year, living her life and learning more about herself along the way. If you feel like you're in a similar rut, then go and watch the cinematic masterpiece that is Avicii's 'I Could Be The One' music video. That video alone brings me joy.

The second thing I value more than ever are my friends and family. Yes, I know this sounds like my Miss Universe speech but, honestly, people need each other. Connection, love and just being A1 to one another can go a long way. Also, I'm not saying you need to see them every day. One of my best friends, Éadin, is like Carmen Sandiego because I never know where in the world she is, but every few months we're able to meet and it's like nothing has changed. I know it's so hard to make friends, especially as you grow older, but it is worth the effort. If you feel like you want to put yourself out there and find new friends, here are some tips:

O   Pay people to like you.

Obviously I'm joking, here are some actual tips:

O   Join group-based hobbies. I went to a sewing class when I first moved to Dublin and I made a few friends from that. I also learned how to make a little skirt, so it was a win-win.

O   Go on friendship dates. Friendships work in the same way as romantic relationships. You need to put in time and effort to make them work. Invite someone you think is cool to an event or for a coffee or a drink. I know it's scary but nine times out of ten the other person would be well up for it.

O   Don't be afraid of walking away if it's not a match. Just like in romantic dating, you may not click with someone and that's okay. There are plenty more friends in the sea. If you feel like the friendship is toxic or one-sided, just strut away, babes.

Like I mentioned earlier, another way I'm starting to find joy in my day-to-day life are my wholesome little hobbies. Being a complete beginner at something will humble you and if, like me, you have a competitive nature, you need to be humbled sometimes. Things I've picked up this year are sewing, yoga, making kombucha and skiing. Yes, I'm cosplaying as a stereotypical suburban trophy wife with a rich husband. Am I good at any of these hobbies? No, but it's fun.

GET IN, GIRLIES, WE'RE DOING A SUMMARY

We hop all over the gaff in this book, but before we go here are some key takeaways from the Mamual that you can start applying to your own life. (Well, if you want. Like, we're not going to force you.)

o   There is no direct path or formula in life.

o   Brunch is the most important meal of the day.

o   Everyone's pretending, so just go for it.

o   Grief is shit, but you will eventually be able to look back on your memories with them and smile.

o   Don't touch the drag queens.

o   There is nothing unnatural about being queer and you will find a community that loves you.

o   Girlbossing and gatekeeping are not the one.

o   Respect the mother figures in your life.

o   A cuppa tea and a chat helps most problems.

o   Sometimes you have to lean into the chaos for the laugh and the story after.

Bye, bye, bye, bye, bye, bye

We hope you've enjoyed reading our stories as much as we've enjoyed sharing them. It really feels like a massive moment for us to be telling these tales that have shaped us into the proud people we are today, when at one point in our lives we were debilitated by the fear of anyone knowing about who we were. Whether you're part of the queer community or not, we hope our stories have highlighted that there is no direct path in life. We're fully aware of how privileged we are to have had such supportive families, and if you haven't been as fortunate as us, remember that a mother's love and wisdom can come from any person within a community. We're all just figuring it out, and the majority of the time people are just pretending to know what's going on, so take everything with a pinch of salt, girlies, and let's be nice to each other.

LGBTQ+ Resources and Being a Better Ally

Though our experiences as queer people in Ireland have largely been positive ones, there's still a lot of work that needs to be done to ensure that the country is safer, more accepting and most importantly equal for all, as bigotry and prejudice still continue to exert their negative legacy on many LGBTQ+ lives in Ireland.

A quick search on GCN, Ireland's longest-running queer online publication, details six separate and serious incidents of homophobic abuse in Ireland in the last year alone. The trans community is constantly under attack in Ireland. We see it every day on Twitter, the mainstream media and even from a failed healthcare system. They are seeking to dehumanise our trans brothers and sisters and it's relentless. Still in Ireland, the majority of children within LGBTQ+ families are prevented from having a legal relationship with both of their parents. This results in many avoidable issues for children as the grow up: medical treatment, school enrolments, foreign travel and tax and inheritance rights. These are just some of the areas that are needlessly complicated when one parent is viewed as a legal stranger to their child. Another disparity comes in the form of giving blood whereby, in Ireland, a man who has had oral or anal sex with another man in the past twelve months is banned from donating, compared to more nuanced criteria for gay blood donors in the UK and many other countries. As we are writing this book there is currently an organised campaign by right-wing groups happening in Ireland to ban queer books. They are targeting public libraries and are trying to incite homophobic and transphobic panic in communities.

There are amazing organisations out there who are combatting the hate and helping the queer community thrive. The following is a list of some of those who are doing extraordinary work in improving the lives of LGBTQ+ people in Ireland.

LGBT IRELAND

LGBT Ireland is a national organisation underpinned by localised knowledge and responses. Together with their network of members, they provide support, training, and advocacy which aims to improve the lives of LGBTQ+ people across Ireland.

BELONG TO

BeLonG To Youth Services is the national organisation supporting LGBTQ+ young people in Ireland. Since 2003 they have worked with LGBTQ+ young people, between 14 and 23 years, to create a world where they are equal, safe and valued in the diversity of their identities and experiences.

They also advocate and campaign on behalf of young LGBTQ+ people, and offer a specialised LGBTQ+ youth service with a focus on mental and sexual health, alongside drug and alcohol support. They respond to the needs of LGBTQ+ young people in Ireland and help them thrive.

TRANSGENDER EQUALITY NETWORK IRELAND – TENI

TENI is a non-profit organisation supporting the trans community in Ireland. TENI seeks to improve the situation and advance the rights and equality of trans people and their families.

EQUALITY FOR CHILDREN

Many children of LGBTQ+ parents in Ireland are denied the right to have a legally recognised relationship with both of their parents. Equality for Children gives a voice to those children and families in their fight for equality by working with LGBT Ireland and other partners.

LGBT PAVEE

LGBT Pavee look to unite those of any age and gender who identify as being LGBTQ+, especially within the Travelling and Roma communities by providing support for those questioning their sexuality.

GAY SWITCHBOARD IRELAND

Gay Switchboard Ireland provides a confidential telephone support service. Their friendly, trained volunteers provide a safe space where listening, support, information and signposting are provided to all callers in a non-directive or judgmental way.

ACT UP DUBLIN AND CORK

ACT UP Dublin and Cork are a diverse, non-partisan group of individuals united in anger and committed to direct action to end the HIV crisis.

HIV IRELAND

HIV Ireland contributes towards a significant reduction in the incidence and prevalence of HIV in Ireland and towards the realisation of an AIDS-free generation by advocating for individuals living with HIV, preventing new HIV infections and combating HIV-related stigma and discrimination.

MPOWER

The MPOWER Programme is a suite of peer-driven community-level interventions, which aim to achieve a reduction in the acquisition of HIV and STIs and an overall improvement of sexual health and well-being among gay, bisexual and other men who have sex with men (gbMSM).

OUTHOUSE

Outhouse provides a safe space, which facilitates and encourages the growth of services and supports to the LGBTQ+ communities.

Here are some other ways you can help the LGBTQ+ community:

o If you hear people making hurtful comments or jokes about LGBTQ+ people, call it out. Let your family, friends or co-workers know that you find it offensive.

o Check your privilege. Being privileged does not mean your life has been an easy one without struggles. That's not what we're getting at. It simply means that you possess some unearned advantage in society through some aspect of your identity. We ourselves are privileged in that we're white, able-bodied, cisgendered men. Acknowledging your privilege in conversations can help marginalised groups feel more comfortable about expressing themselves and you can then utilise your own privilege to help the lives of oppressed groups.

o Being an ally is an action, not a label. You need to be proactive in your support and it should be consistent.

o Don't be afraid of getting things wrong. We all make mistakes. Learn from them and let those mistakes make you into a better person. If you happen to use the incorrect pronouns for a person simply apologise and make a concerted effort to get it right in future.

o Listen and learn. Listen to the stories of your queer friends and learn about their experiences. Research LGBTQ+ history and find out about the struggles we once faced and still face today.

o Tell your friends to buy this book, x.

Acknowledgements

To all the team at Gill Books, especially Seán, Fiona, Aoibheann and Djinn. Writing a book has been no easy feat, but your belief in our work spurred us on and helped keep the imposter syndrome at bay.

To our extremely talented illustrator, Alannah. Thank you for bringing our stories to life with your drawings. You are so good at what you do. We're beyond grateful that you've been a part this book and a part of our podcast.

To all the girls at The Collaborations Agency for looking after us and helping manage our other commitments while we focused on the book. We're mad about ye.

PJ

A huge thank you to my siblings: Lindsey, Elaine, Martina, Gary, Mike and Stephen. You're all hilarious storytellers in your own right and I wouldn't be the person I am today, or be able to take a slagging, without your guidance from an early age.

To my friends who have been a constant support, the stars in my stories and a springboard for new ideas. I'd be lost with you.

To all the queer people who have come before me and fought for our right to exist. Look at us now, writing books about our experiences. None of this would be possible without you.

Thank you to Sailor Moon and Happy for being my emotional-support cats. Stay iconic.

To Jose for your constant love and support throughout all of this. Your unique ability to calm me and get to the root of my emotions is infuriating at times but absolutely necessary. You constantly inspire me to be as authentic and open as I can be, and I promise to try to do the same for you for years to come. Love always endures.

And last but not least, to the legend herself, Nuls. I feel so lucky to have a mam that has taught me how to lead with my heart in every aspect of my life. A mam to not just me but any friend that I brought into our home. None of this would be possible without you. I love you so much. Coffees on me for the foreseeable.

Kevin

To my siblings, Shane, Robert and Sarah. I know it can't be easy having a brother as unreal as myself, but you all handle yourselves with such grace.

Sarah, thanks for telling me I'm not funny because it only made me more determined to make you laugh.

Robert, your funny stories in the back of the car on the way to Kerry when we were kids are some of my earliest memories of laughter.

Shane, thanks for paying my rent when I was broke in London and didn't want to ask Mam and Dad for the money. It was one of the nicest things someone has ever done for me.

To Pádraig. We've been living out of each other's pockets since the day we met and I wouldn't have it any other way. I feel so lucky that we got to tackle things together growing up; it made me feel a bit invincible. I knew that we'd be okay because we had each other. I'm glad that other people will get to laugh at our stories.

To the staff at Clarnico Coffee Club, who catered to my caffeine needs whilst I was writing this book. The countless oat milk flat whites were always made with love. Thank you for being a dog-friendly coffee shop because having cute dogs appear at random intervals in the day was such a welcome distraction from staring at my laptop. If you're reading this, please bring back the peanut butter blondies.

To Furq. You've been like a mentor to me since we first met, but more importantly you've been an incredible friend. I'm so glad our paths crossed when they did and I can't wait for the world to see you flourish.

To Laura de Barra. Your advice has been invaluable to me, and your WhatsApp voice notes always have me howling. You're an absolute gem.

Mam, you really are my best friend. One of the reasons I got into a habit of telling funny stories is because I love to see you laugh. Thank you for your unconditional love and for passing your beautiful long eyelashes on to me. I love you to the moon and back and around the world and back again.